Foundations of Library and Information Science

Foundations of Library and Information Science

Dr. P. Balasubramanian
M.A., M.B.A., M.C.A., M.L.I.Sc., M.Phil., PGDPR, Ph.D.
University Librarian & Head
Department of Library & Information Science
Manonmaiam Sundaranar University
Tirunelveli 627012
Tamil Nadu
India

Ess Ess Publications
New Delhi

Foundations of Library and Information Science

ISBN : 978-93-87698-29-1
Price : Rs. 925/-

First Published 2021

Published by:
Ess Ess Publications
4831/24, Ansari Road,
Darya Ganj,
New Delhi-110 002.
INDIA
Phones: 23260807, 41563444
Fax: 41563334
E-mail: info@essessreference.com
www.essessreference.com

Cover Design by *Patch Creative Unit*

Printed and bound in India

Dedicated to
MY BELOVED PARENTS

Contents

Contents

Preface

As library has gained more exposure and importance in the current century, it had more growth in the revolution of information. In this **"Foundation of Library and Information Science"** book, main objective is to get knowledge about importance of having a Libraries/Information center.

Here in the book we have discussed about concept, methods and implication regarding foundation of libraries and Information center. Subject that matter is discussed with Basic English so that the readers can get better understanding.

To make it valuable I gave my complete effort. Throughout, the whole book has been written with the readers in mind. I hope who goes through it will find it interesting and worth reading. I do not expect everybody to agree with the content and ideas put forth in this book.

But I do hope that the knowledge and information offered will become a wake-up call for most people.

I acknowledge my heartfelt gratitude to Dr. P. Ravichandaran, Professor and Head, Department of Library and Information Science, Annamalai University, Annamalai Nagar for invaluable advice and suggestions.

Finally, I would like to acknowledge the pleasure of working with publishing team of ESS ESS Publication, New Delhi.

— **Dr. P. Balasubramanian**

Acknowledgements

The author feels extremely indebted to Dr. K. Pitchumani, Hon'ble Vice-Chancellor, Manonmaniam Sundaranar University, Tirunelveli. We also thank Dr. S. Santhosh Baboo, Registrar, Manonmaniam Sundaranar University, Tirunelveli and all the teaching and non-teaching staff members of the M.S. University, for giving us constant encouragement for writing this book.

We would be a benefit killer if we do not acknowledge the services of ESS Publications, New Delhi for their efforts in bringing out this book in a record time. Suggestions for further improvement of the book are most welcome.

— **Dr. P. Balasubramanian**

1
Introduction to Library

LEARNING OBJECTIVES

After studying this unit, you will be able to:
- Identify libraries' significance.
- Analyze the need for government libraries to be established.
- Identify the values, morality and key of library scheme.
- Knowledge of different data bodies.
- Knowledge of significances of multiple library and legislation.
- Explain socio-economic growth.
- Explain libraries role in the growth of education.

The library is places where group of people can be created, collected, updated, and manage information. A list of documents and important file data is displayed by each library, so that individuals can work together using documents.

LIS, a research of the manufacture, dissemination, discovery, evaluation, selection, acquisition, use, organization, maintenance and management of data carriers is the scholarly and professional study. This book aims to bring readers in the field of library and information studies to basic interests and evolving discussions.

A secondary objective of this book is to present the publication in the field of bibliography to prominent authors, papers and books. The book was created as annotations of key I IS papers.

1.1. LIBRARY & SOCIETY: ROLE OF LIBRARIES IN SOCIO-ECONOMIC CULTURAL AND EDUCATIONAL DEVELOPMENT

Libraries play a basic role in society as gateways to information and culture. These resources and facilities generate learning possibilities, promote literacy and education and contribute to the shaping of fresh concepts and views that are essential to a creative and innovative community. It also helps to guarantee that the information produced and accumulated by previous generations is genuine. In a world without libraries, research and human understanding would be hard to advance or maintain for future generations the cumulative information and history of the world.

A library depict various things to people from a location where mothers can bring children and learners can study to read their first stories to a service that allows anyone to purchase a book, have Internet access or do research. Libraries merely give a way to gain access to information.

Libraries stand for education and give innumerable possibilities of learning that can create financial, social and cultural growth.

1.1.1. Preserving Cultural Heritage

Mahatma Gandhi, who recognizes the cultural significance of sharing, said, "No culture can live if it tries to be exclusive." Information and knowledge are encouraged to share and recycle in many ways. The desire to maintain our culture for the coming generations is perhaps the deepest of our human instincts. This is one of the most significant job of a library.

Libraries are best sources of historically and culturally significant collections, many of which are not available anywhere else in the world. Without an appropriate copyright exception, a library could not preserve or replace a damaged work while it is still covered by copyright. For example, an old newspaper or a unique sound recording to preserve it could not be legally copied or digitized. This cultural heritage would be lost to future generations without suitable library exceptions.

Many works are now "born digital" only and are not available in print form, such as websites or electronic publications. Without legal means of conservation and replacement of works of art in a range of media and formats, including format transfer and migration from outdated storage formats many of these works will inevitably be lost to historians for future generations.

1.1.2. Socio-Economic Development

A data society, as stated above, is the way to get data from one location to another. As technology is progressing over time, so have we adjusted the manner in which we share the data within ourselves.

"Second Nature" relates to a group of cultural experiences. They get refurbished in something else which can take on a fresh significance. As a community, we turn this process into a natural thing for us, i.e. second nature. Therefore, we can acknowledge how we are using and move data in distinct ways by pursuing a specific pattern generated by culture. All of this has become a usual method, which we as a community accept for sure, from exchanging data via various time zones to data in another place. By shared data vectors, however, we have been able to further disseminate data. The data can migrate and then distance itself from the original items which allowed it to progress through the use of these vectors.

From here has created something known as "third nature." Second nature expansion, third nature is second nature controlled. It can mold fresh and distinct methods of informing. Third nature can therefore speed up, proliferate, split, mutate and radiate from other places. It is aimed at balancing space and time limits. It's seen in the telegraph, the first successful technology that could send and receive information faster than an object could be moved by a person. As a consequence, various vectors of human beings have the capacity not only to shape culture but eventually generate fresh opportunities to shape society. Consequently, society can make use of the second nature and the third nature to explore new ways of creating new types of communication by molding data.

1.1.3. The Role of Libraries in Educational Development

Education is described as a complex of social procedures, officially or otherwise, to acquire expertise and experience. Ogunsheye (1981) says that the complete apparatus used for the individual's growth is involved. The library provides the person with the chance of reading and therefore of interacting with the riches and acquired information of the society in a manner spiritual, inspiring and pleasant. The library can be regarded as a training extension.

Library facilities are necessary for maintaining the abilities that the provision of excellent literature has gained through literacy courses. To make education more effective in shaping and constructing a happier person and a better society, suppliers of education have a more practical role to play in offering libraries for maintaining the newly gained abilities of adult learners than their role of literacy facilitators. The organization of a library requires a friendly environment and a helpful collection to support education. Bookstore training should be provided to facilitators involved in the planning of training programs, and students guiding process.

The two inseparable concepts "Education" and "Library," both essentially and synchronously linked to each other and coexist. You cannot separate one from the other. None of them is an end in itself; they are both a means to an end. One of them dies when the other dies. One survives while the other is alive. This inter-relation and coexistence, if you like, has been a method of evolution in accordance with the multiple requirements, changes and situations at the multiple phases of human existence, from the birth of man's civilization to the posterity.

A fresh vision for UNESCO's sustainable development agenda is the notion of education and its relationship with Education for All (EFA). The United Nations Decade on Education for Sustainable Development was adopted in December 2002 by the United Nations General Assembly and UNESCO was appointed as the lead agency to promote the Decade. In December 2002, UNESCO adopted Resolution 57/254.

In fact, the development, through the United Nations Literacy Decade (UNLD) and the Millennium Development Goals (MDGs), of the concept of sustainable development education and its relation to education for all (EFA) clearly illustrates that quality education, as a bibliography objective, is a prerequisite for sustainable development education, both at the different levels and in all forms. The UNESCO education policies and plans for schooling and its growth, poverty reduction, universal human values and tolerance and fresh ICTs (library) difficulties. Educational policies and plans for schooling and their growth.

Development of education is a Web definition of the method of enhancing the efficiency of education by continuously reviewing appropriate variables at all levels, from teaching methods and equipment to organizational structures and policies, and by providing processes for progressive change.

1.1.4. Library in Recreation and Leisure

The healthy use of recreation is an important thing in community life, in order to prevent adverse and harmful actions from occurring during leisure. The library addresses its users ' recreational requirements through the storage of appropriate books. The main subjects of the book or leisure are novels and other types of literature, art, travel books, biographies, famous journals, etc. and they should be placed in every library.

In addition to its standard role in schooling, culture, religion, religious research, and so on, the library's function in contemporary technocratic society has expanded considerably to modifications happening in the various facets of human life, which may be briefly stated as follows:

1. Social stress : Pressure on population, increased urbanization, rural growth, population mobility, dynamic groups and pressure, etc.;

2. Economic : Work patterns, incomes, prices, values, inflation, dynamic development, macro and micro-economic trends, etc.

3. Political : Political structures and systems, political party, legislatures and parliamentary operations and parliamentary assemblies, structure of power etc.;

4. Educational : Educational and instructional materials, education technology, etc., at all levels of formal and informal learning and education;

5. Research and development : Scientific, technological, social, information development, innovation, dissemination, dissemination, distribution and use, technology transfer, etc.;

6. Industry and business : Production and distribution, acquisition of technology, evaluation and implementation, marketing and sales and so on;

7. Trade and commerce : Import and export, trade and global business, etc.

8. Government and administration : Planning, policy development, execution and administration etc.

9. Cultural : Fine arts, music, entertainment, film, broadcast, etc.

1.1.5. Expanding Role of Library

The standard functions of the library were dramatically modified by all these variables. A number of operations based on paperwork and data analysis, consolidation and repackaging, computer, information systems, etc. must meet the user's current data requests. In the recent three decades, interesting new kinds of organizations have emerged together with the Library, such as documentation centers, information analytics centers, databases, resources centers, multimedia centers, etc. Many of these innovations have also given fresh possibilities for marketing data goods and services, thus paving the way for a growing data sector.

1.1.5.1. The role of the Higher education

The following roles are as below:

- Education support.
- Teaching research and training in society through access to information resources, materials and references.
- Information dissemination and distribution.
- Knowledge stored for stakeholders in training in such documents.
- The gateways to global library collections.
- Informal self-education and education support.

1.1.5.2. Roles of User education

- Create healthy habits by reading.
- Literacy information, computer literacy.
- Encourage the use of collections and facilities of libraries.

1.1.5.3. The roles of the Recreation

- Educational, municipal and cultural support.
- Group and organizational activities.

1.1.5.4. The role of the Library as a place

- Commons information in the learning library model.
- To provide a building designed architecturally as a place that inspires everyone's interest in academic work.

1.1.5.5. The role of the Societal and Cultural

- Democratizing information and knowledge in society
- Linking people to sources of knowledge and information
- Raising awareness among underprivileged sections of society of the social and economic development opportunities in society.
- Information resources for the Community.
- Community awareness of government programs like mass literacy.
- Organization of cultural activities for social harmony, such as book debates, lectures on key topics.
- Support for civic and cultural activities by organizations and groups.
- Conservation of knowledge for posterity.
- Traditional knowledge collection and preservation.
- Serving as a gateway to national and local authorities.

1.1.6. Technical supports

In particular for non-English and for old materials and fonts, we have to improve the tools for the digitization and indexing of texts. Advances in technological tools can help to reduce costs and increase digitization efficiency. In order to accomplish that, we need to combine the expertise in Member States with the various stakeholder communities–companies, libraries and archives, universities and research organizations. In real competence centers interdisciplinary cooperation can help us advance digital technology worldwide.

The users of digital libraries want the most precise and complete answers to their inquiries to easy-to-find materials, without having to navigate through results or screen data pages. That means that the resources required for digital libraries in the fields of information and communication technologies, audio, visually, multimedia, radio frequency technology and smart cards, etc., will be much more sophisticated and automatic.

1.1.7. The Change of Society

The users of the library are children, adults, teenagers, seniors, etc. Online access to electronic documents, e-journals, e-theses, e-papers etc. is provided via the internet. The communication was communicated via e-mail, Facebook social networks, Twitter, Linked In, etc. The ideas shared, the tube downloaded and downloaded etc. Save the reader's time and get the information from the library. The company's library changes are cultural, the reading circle, the forum for readers, etc.

1.2. INFORMATION INSTITUTIONS OF DIFFERENT KINDS: LIBRARIES, ARCHIVES, DOCUMENTATION CENTRES, INFORMATION ANALYSIS CENTRES, MUSEUMS AND THEIR RESPECTIVE ROLES AND FUNCTIONS

There are different types of traditional information institutions according to the literature. The most popular types of information include: libraries, documentation centers, information analytics centers, data centers, etc. Apart from these long-established traditional institutions which provide information support to individuals and other institutions, many de-institutionalized information services have emerged lately. The following sections of the unit discuss some of the important types of information institutions.

The KBE concepts and the consequential changes required by information institutions to prepare for the new competitive era have been mentioned. The new Knowledge Economy as a period of rapid change, Chase's (1998) forecast, is also discussed-a paradigm change of information institutions.

1.2.1. Libraries

The stories of his death, which appeared in New York papers when he lived in London in 1897, were squeezed with that brief rejoinder Mark Twain. Unfortunately, equally false killing reports of libraries published in the press since the 1960s are not easy to squeeze out. The truth of the matter is that libraries are well-lived and adaptable to the world. Despite the ravages of inflation and budget cuts, they continue to serve millions of thankful users in both old and new ways. It is true that various new and costly business information services are mushrooming to serve business and industry's specific needs, but for most of us, libraries will be and will still be the only affordable on-city or campus information game (Richard De Gennaro) for years to come. In a rapidly accelerating series of developments in the technology which multiplies its power, while drastically cutting costs. The current prediction is that electronic technology will soon replace books and libraries. These included satellite communication, cable TV, low cost optical and digital video mass storage and powerful microcomputers on chips.

We acquire a technology level with them that fires imagination and creates even the most imaginative expectations! In such a heated environment, there is a risk, in favor of more glamorous alternatives to promising but not yet tested technologies that those responsible for the financial support of libraries will neglect or early give up traditional libraries.

There are impressive credentials for the experts who predict the early death of books and libraries. These include managers, information entrepreneurs, government officials, professors from universities and popular futurists. Their forecasts of what lies ahead are based on solid expertise and years of experience. They cannot be ignored or uncritically accepted. In theory book and future scientists, the insights and perspectives are useful; they help us to understand, but only the authoritative and responsible ones can decide how and when these forces may affect a particular enterprise. The social, economic and technological forces are complex in a wider environment. Futurists can tell us how the future could be, but they can't tell us how or when to get there. At the end of the day, those responsible must make the truly important decisions regarding any organization or institution on the basis of their best judgment and practice as much as possible. Among those who predict an early end in books and libraries are Dr. F.W.Lancaster and Dr. Vincent E. Giuliano, prominent and representative.

Lancaster sums up his views as follows:

"We are moving towards a paperless society rather quickly and inevitably. Advances in computer science and communications technology enable us to design an overall system that compiles, publishes and uses research and development reports in fully electronic format. In this communication environment, paper never needs to be available. We are currently in an interim stage in the natural development of print on paper and electronic materials. "If Lancaster thinks about paperless society that is only a small part of a big change in our society and way of life. Of course, it can also become obsolete in society, not only libraries, but also the institutions and scientists they serve. The best thing we can do is try to tackle the changes coming here in the next 10 or 15 years and try to plan for those coming when books and papers can definitely exist in conjunction with electronic media.

It is also important to note that the World Wide Web (WWW) changes the face of libraries, how they are utilized and appreciated. Whether the library wishes it or not, the WWW shall have a major effect on the library. This effect would largely be dictated by technologically and socially based forces to the library. As a consequence of Internet and WWW technology, libraries now have software instruments to overcome certain restrictions related to the absence of connection between the overall primary user frame setting and library resources on a distinct device or machine. The WWW can overcome the absence of characteristics to find data in the overall user main frame environment and can also generate the virtual "site" where customers (users) can readily find an electronic presence-a starting point for library services. In reality, WWW offers the tool for the integration of other technologies in the library as well as fresh resources and facilities, such as online catalogs and searchable texts. It is notable that WWW is a technology that could characterize the bibliographical end, as we understand it today. With or without library involvement, it will certainly affect. What becomes of the library is still unclear, as a technology often takes many years to get through. Library consumers already expect a lot from their libraries, most important of which is enhanced access to all types of data, plus much greater self-service. In light of the fast pace of changes in technology and society today, we can see that changes in technology can force social change on society and its institutions.

Viewed from this point, the library of the next few decades will be;

(i) A place where people will not come as the data resources physically.

(ii) Become a facilitator for access.

(iii)   Coordinate access to digital resources locally constructed.

In closing the chapter on libraries, it should be emphasized that the stereotype of libraries is no longer applicable as static, constant organizations, they must be able to develop, adapt to evolving circumstances to satisfy new needs and execute new techniques. If these aspects are taken into account, the predictions of their future existence do not need to be taken into consideration.

1.2.2. Archives

The archival terms most frequently used are those describing documents and organizations. Documentary materials may, on the grounds of who created and kept documents and for what end, be classified as "records," "private papers" or "artificial collection." The records are in any form that a public agency, church, company, the university or other institution produces or receives and maintains. In general, copies of letters, memorandums, reports, reports and photographs, and other materials produced by the organization and input letters, reports, memorandum received from other offices and other records in the files of the organization may also be included in the records of an organization.

In comparison to the documents, a person or family in the process of living creates or receives and maintains private documents. The materials typically used in private documents include journals, news clippings, private economic documents, photos, correspondence obtained, and copies of written and sent letters by a person or family.

Traditionally, documents and private documents, each having obviously definable features, are regarded separate entities. The physical characteristics of documents and private documents became more similar in the twentieth century but rather their differences, archivists emphasized more and more the similarities between these materials. In specific, the archivist today acknowledges that documents as well as private documents are interconnected bodies of materials which have been brought together for function or use. In organizations of documents and in private documents, archivists respect and pursue the established relationships among individual items.

Depending on the type of documentary material they contain and the way in which it is obtained, archives may be called "archives or" manuscript repositories. "Archives" have traditionally been the long-term care facilities of the organization or institution for which they belong. Many public archives are accountable for documents of a government or public body's ongoing importance. Examples of government archives at domestic level are the US National Archives and the Public Archives of Canada. There are also public archives on each other's level of government, including state or province, county or municipality. The records of any other instituti n or organization of which they are a party shall be maintained by no public or non-governmental archives. For instance, church archives administer the documents of a congregation or religious denomination. The archives of the university are accountable for the administration documents of the university. Archives obtain historical material by law or by inner institutional or policy regulation.

Manuscript repositories' are mainly private paper archival institutions, artificial collections and documents of others. Repository manuscripts buy or seek donations to products they do not need. They must therefore document material transfers by donation certificate or by other legal agreement.

The differences between archives and repositories of manuscripts could be made clear. However, few archival institutions are merely "archives," or "manuscript repositories." Even a tiny group of donated personal papers and non-government documents is liable for the US National Archives. Many repositories of manuscripts serve likewise as the archives of their respective organizations. In recognition of this, for some archivists, the term« archives» has gradually gained more significance and is used for any organization of archive purposes. The use of the term' archives' in the name of certain organizations, which might previously have been referred to as' handwritten repositories,' has enhanced this fashion.

1.2.3. Documentation Centers

Documentation Centers are very essential among the various types of organization used to collect and disseminate documentary data. Libraries have traditionally performed the fundamental role of gathering and keeping every publication in a re idy-to-use condition. The impetus for providing documentation facilities for expert consumers has emerged following World War II, primarily as a result of exponential development and the complexities of data sources. This resulted in demand for services, which involved analyzing in detail the material of the library holdings. In other words, the focus was on providing data contained in papers instead of sending them. The fresh generation of organizations, known as documentation centres, was paved the way for this scenario. A fundamental function of any documentation center is that it informs specialized users about the latest and existing value literature. The tasks allocated to a documentation center differ from Documentation center to Documentation Centre. For instance, a local documentation center can offer data services to help its parent organization's operations and programs. It would gather and serve data about the institution's real job. In order to achieve this goal, the choice and purchase of worthwhile content and its organization can be done by the local Documentation Centre. Their services can be intended to meet their users 'current and expected requirements. In other words, both anticipatory services as well as services intended to meet the particular needs of customers could be supplied by the local documentation center. On the other side, a domestic documentation center will carry out certain rest tasks and may carry out operations outside the means of local documentation centers.

Local Documentation Centers are generally linked with and administered by the parent organizations of individual R&D organizations, companies, industrial companies and public agencies etc. In many instances, a division of the primary establishment would be the Documentation Centre. At domestic level, the establishment and administration of such a center may be the duty of the relevant public organizations. The general rule suggested in relation to economic aid is that 5% of the budget spent on R&D should be transferred to the national center's expenses. Documentation centers are mainly set up by the government in a developing nation like India.

In distinct nations, there are distinct models of organization. There have been centralized and decentralized buildings. Countries such as Great Britain have a combination of centralized and decentralized designs. However, in the contemporary age, the network idea has acquired momentum and the trend is to pool and share resources for maximum economics and efficiency.

1.2.4. Information Analysis Centers

The Weinberg Report addressed the function and significance of data analysis centers and highlighted that "science and technology are inherent to the operations of the most effective (data analysis) centers. Not only do the centers disseminate and collect data, they generate fresh data. The method of transferring big amounts of information often leads to fresh generalizations. In brief, the skilled scientist that can collect appropriate data, examine the field and distill information in ways that go to the core of a technical scenario is more helpful than just a stack of the appropriate papers. The expert is overburdened. These knowledgeable interlocutors who add themselves to sciences are the cornerstone of the Information Center (analysis); rather than a technical library, they create the Information Centre. It consists of extremely qualified researchers and technicians who see the operation of the center as a way of developing and strengthening their private contact with their science and technology.

This extensive definition was written in the COSATI standing panel, A data analysis center is a specific, (but not necessarily solely) officially organized organizational unit developed in order to acquire, select, store, retrieve, assess, analyze and synthesize, A body of data and/or a obviously defined field of information or a specific task intended to compile, digest, repackage or otherwise organize and present the most authentic, timely, and helpful to a colleagues and management society relevant information and/or data.

IACs are mainly involved in the following operations: analysis, interpretation, synthesis, assessment and repackaging of data by experts in subject matter, leading in fresh information being produced, assessed in the form of critical examinations, state-of-the-art monographs, and compilations of data as well as meaningful, evaluated questions, which help to enhance the user community. The diagram shows the primary work of a typical IAC.

Activities	Product
Selection and Collection of Document/Information	Bibliographies, Current Awareness
Abstracting/Indexing	Indexed Bibliographies, Custom Searches
Extracting	Descriptive Reviews, Compilation (unevaluated)
Evaluation	Critical Compilation of Data
	Criteria for Experimentation Recommendations
	Solutions to (Immediate) Problems
	Correlation of Data
	Prediction of Properties

(*Source* : Atherton, 1977)
Fig. 1. Activities and Products of
Information Analysis Centres

1.2.5. Museum

The main objective is the development of the collection consisting of selection, acquisition and conservation. They maintain the collections and provide customers instead of borrowing for observation.

There is a great deal of information in the objects and collections that compose the university museums that can tell some histories. Specimens of learning are used to illustrate special topics and disciplines while contributing to modern studies, especially in life sciences, archaeology and history. Furthermore, they assist to shape the university's higher legacy. The college is one of the oldest and most distinctive collective organizations, but the story of the college Museum provides little indication of the current or previous connection of the college collections to the parent organization. While university museums address the historical and progressive growth of a specified topic or discipline, if the university is present, its significant and active function is greatly understood. These objects constitute the study of the university that leads to countless breakthroughs and findings of the world of today.

Potentially, the collection standards, the equipment accessible and on site knowledge of university museums are accessible to provide a progressive museum service in accordance with their future-oriented university environment. In general, however, university museums do not have enough money, the room necessary to store, study and show their collections, as well as suited personnel requirements. Once considered a' model' for the contemporary museum, the university museum has lost decades of development, reconciliation and reorganization, perhaps over the last 30 years, without any initial novelty.

1.2.5.1. *The crises of the 20th century university museum*

In the 1980s and 1990s, government cuts in government expenditure and structu al changes in greater schooling led to staff scarcity and efforts to rationalize the collection of universities through disposal and sale. These modifications coincided with modifications to the teaching based on objects. As teaching has changed dramatically in terms of both content and methodology, the interests of studies have shifted and previously used collections have become precarious, unemployed.

Furthermore, university funds were transferred from collection to teachers and student recruitment and new research and related equipment expanded. The community of the museum asked about the modern role of the collections of universities. In 1986 the Manchester Museum Director, Alan Warhurst, describes the college museum's fight as a "crisis of identity and purpose, crisis of acceptance, which is compounded by a crisis of funds".

Universities' museums have been required to "secure their own parent organizations, both internally and for society, and importance of their collection."

1.2.5.2. The changing role of the 21st century university museum

The collections created by universities are some of the oldest, rarest, and most significant artifacts. University museums have the ability to differentiate themselves from other museums. The collections provide material proof for the progress of the university's education and understanding, as well as its educational and cultural importance for the general public. Universities can distinguish with other museums by recognizing and selecting to show their organizational heritage and Boylan says, "Giving the importance of public relations to the external image of the university." (Boylan 1999) In addition to offering a' triple mission,' the acknowledged institutional heritage of universities may be granted to university museums. This gradual strategy to the collection and display of universities also covers the archaic perception of university museums. Like the university itself, the university museum also remains important during the 21st century and still recognizes its early foundations, combining a medieval psychological tradition and involvement in modern science.

1.2.5.3. Institutional heritage recognition and the university museum

Institutional heritage recognition is not a fresh idea. Its external picture was articulated through its material patrimony from the medieval foundation of the university. In addition to the educational purpose, architecture, collections and libraries differentiated certain universities for their high-profile assets and a significantly constructed atmosphere. Touring scientists and visitors have long been hosted by universities, as the early type of promotion or recruitment in institutions. Universities have provided bookstores, curiosity offices, photo galleries and college spaces for institutional advancement as part of these visits. Rawson at the University of St Andrews (Ecosse's oldest university) claims that some items have frequently been shown to tourists as part of the standardized university trip, and the display of these products not only convey the valuable objects owned by the University but they also convey data about the importance that attach to its own history, pride in its associate. (Rawson 2004).s

This identity recognition shows the university's appreciation of the importance of identity. The college had items and collections that it had acknowledged as important in forming its identity, previous and present, already before the foundation of the college museum in St Andrews.

The collections of universities quickly extended during the 18th and 19th centuries, partially to affirm this concept of institutional identity but mainly to promote object-based education. Institutions have sought to provide the most extensive and useful study examples for their teachers and learners, and certain global subjects such as the frozen Dodo stuffed from the 17th century once exhibited in Oxford's Ashmolean Museum as an integral part of the Commercial Coll ction. In the form of study collection, documents, facilities and private objects, teachers and scholars made contributions to university collections as well. Dr. John Woodward, the founder of Dr. John Woodward's collection of natural and archeological samples of history, is still preserved at Cambridge's Sedgwick Museum of Earth Sciences. The College Maius maintains a number of pictures of the Polish astronomer Copernicus at the Jagellonian University Museum in Krakow, featuring a distinctive collection of tools from the 15th century including a heavenly world and several amazons. In addition to the didactics of these artifacts and collections, they form the material identity of the university and the museum to which they belong in their respective educational departments. They also serve as concrete proof of the development of understanding and teaching which has taken place during the time span and continues to this day.

1.2.5.4. Universities and university museums: reflexive responsibilities

The university is an organization that is vibrant and constantly changing and whose objects and collections chart and reflect this progress to date. Is it not the university museum's duty to recognize the university's existence and value in its exhibits? Reflecting on the question of the institutional promotion role of its museum in education, research and displays is it not just as important for the university to understand and appreciate. A lot has been written about the university's obligations towards its museum, but what does the museum give in exchange? University museums are anticipated to deliver a greater and more direct service towards their parent organization in the increasingly market-driven world of higher education. (Boylan 2002) University museums can not only display items and collections that are specific to their organizations, but also use them as an illustration of their university tale in recapturing the spirit of institutions ' own identity (Boylan 2002).

As previously stated, university museums have the potential to provide innovative services that immediately benefits the university in terms of institutional awareness and promotion, but also provide the wider audience with the distinctively academic and experimental programs only a university museum can provide. In adopting the term Lourenço, "Musée d'histoire, museums and collections, artifacts and historiques and used in books and records, structures and gardens in short, space and time, form and function, tangible and intangible," University museums are able to behave as innovating histories by taking up a "Multilevel and Integrated Approach" (Lourenço in press). He also illustrates that this inclusion may be' a collection of physical inclusion under one roof or institutional integration,' or both. (Lourenço 2004) The administrative issue to be solved individually is whether or not a centralized space or unit strategy is taken. (Lourenço 2004) The gathering of the collections under the same roof does not ensure an integrated strategy.

1.2.5.5. Physical integration

The combination of the former Helsinki University Museum with the University's History and the Museum of Medical History in 2003 led in the new Museum of the University of Helsinki in the Arppeanum building, which is part of the historic construction of the University of Helsinki in 2003. The collections included the founding material of the university, an imposing series of dental chairs and reconstruction of facilities, and a' magic cup.' A majority of the items appear in the Arppeanum's original cabinets, and are sympathetically treated with modern fittings and lighting. Although disparate collections have been integrated into an historical building at the University of Helsinki museum, the outcome is cohesive and entirely contemporary. By recognizing the capacity of university collections to tell a larger history, the Arppeanum displays not only address the development of individual subjects, but also how they assist to shape the larger identity of universities.

1.2.5.6. The future of university museums

A more inclusive strategy, focused on an individual institutional identity, can offer college museums an interesting fresh position for the 21st century: recognition of institutional heritage. The presence and connection of the university to its museum are not clear enough in exhibits and description, and as Lourenço says, "exceptional potential is created because of the situation of museums at the university, of the university, and for the university " the museum should be active in the university's presence as a parent organization and, most of all, as a "collector." (At press Lourenço)

1.2.6. Data Centers

The modern society needs information in all spheres of human progress for different activities, such as planning, development, decision-making, etc. In order to facilitate the efficient use, the data needs to be collected, processed and organized. There are various categories of data: scientific, technical, technological, industrial, manpower, socioeconomic and demographic data, etc. There are several different types of information. Normally data are collected through the monitoring and surveying process. It is necessary to store and make available to those who need data collected from different sources by different methods. Adequate institutional mechanisms have been developed for this purpose. They are referred to as data centers.

Under UNESCO "the Data Center is an organization for the management of numerical quantitative data". The primary function of these centers is to collect, organize and diffuse data (mostly numerical), and to provide a measurement service, and to advance the corresponding methods. In exchange, the term ' data centers,' not all critical data evaluators, is used to define types of information centers. The scope and size of data centers may differ. Data centers may be located at locally, nationally, regionally and internationally. In general, the data center consists of three main components:

1. Organized collection of data (i.e., the database);
2. A link to the sources that supply the database; and
3. A contact with users who will interact with the database from a different point of view.

This can be diagrammatically represented as:

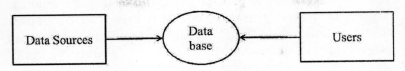

Fig. 2

Structure of a Data Centre : The basic principles for the organization of a data center are as follows:

(i) Data received and collected from the various papers by a specialist group, which determine, control and adapt to the generator source the data's importance and relevance.

(ii) The data received are organized to establish that they provide basic data to be processed or synthetic data to be used in its original form.

(iii) The data are converted and structured for computer processing in machine-readable form.

It can be stated here that the Data Centre's activities may include:

(i) Collection of data,

(ii) Controlling data,

(iii) Codification of data,

(iv) Organization of data and structuring into a database, and

(v) Retrieval of data.

A data center should be equipped with adequately trained workforce to perform all these functions. Under the former NISSAT program, many Data Centers have been established. The National Crystallography Information Center is a best Data Center example.

1.2.7. Referral Centers and Clearing Houses

1.2.7.1. Referral Centers

Various organizations participate in the activity of dissemination. These organizations, for their effective functioning, must be properly coordinated by an agency. This has paved the way for the creation of a new organization called the Referral Centre. Referral centers offer methods for switching between different types of information institutions. A Referral Centre's basic function is to act as a mediator for those who have inquiries on scientific and technical subjects, for organizations and for people with specialized expertise in these areas and are willing to share their knowledge with others. Referral Centers provide guidance and support to the user community on the appropriate information in solving information problems. A referral center must carry out certain fundamental operations to achieve this goal.

1.   An inventory of all major data resources in various fields should be available from a Referral Centre.

2.   The science and technical data resources directories should be compiled and published.

3.   An operational connection within the science data complex must be analyzed by a referral center.

The data resources may include professional companies, the University Research Bureau and Institutes, public agencies, libraries and test stations, and individual professionals as well as more specialist sources of data such as technical libraries, information and documentation centers as well as abstracting and indexing facilities, for the purposes of the referral center.

Any reference center should be in a position at any specific stage to provide data on the amount and place of libraries and specialist data centers. This analytical information will assist with a reference center's day-to-day work.

By letters, private visits and telephone, you may obtain any request for a referral center. In cases of telephone inquiry and private visits, advice may be provided locally, but a letter is usually accompanied by conformity or a complement to the data given. The data provided might be a list of resources names and addresses that match the user's application.

1.2.7.2. Clearing Houses

A Clearing House is a key organization for data collection, classification and distribution. It may include specialized information centers and standard libraries. A clearing house is a fairly fresh term in science language. It constitutes a storehouse for documents with the further purpose of serving the data distribution agency as a key agency. It also involves the collection and retaining of research and development documents. Subjective questions about things in these documents are sometimes referred to the source and may have to operate as a reference center in a Clearing House. As a clearing-house for ongoing studies, Smithsonian Institute of Science Information Exchange Services serves. Similarly, the Library of Congress National Referral Center offers professionals in the field of investigation with reference services. The information or records are not supplied. The Defense Documentation Center in the United States is a storage facility for the Department of Defense's reports and other documents. It also serves as a reference center in which experts in different areas are identified.

Another center that operates as a resource center providing reference service is the Education Research Information Centre. The BLLD, UK, has served as a referral center for several years.

Most Clearing Houses have specialized collections and developed them. They have networks of data to obtain records in their fields. In some chosen fields, they provide specialized data services. They answer particular and general questions and can serve as key research sites for research and development reports in particular.

1.2.8. Deinstitutionalized Information Services

The following sections have discussed briefly various

kinds of traditional information institutions. The objective was to give some concept about the spectrum of information institutions set up for the requirements of information for society over a period of time. The library, as the traditional stockroom of information and the conservation of cultural patrimony, was also indicated to fall in the midst of the transformation caused by technological developments. If this change is accepted, the essence of institutionalized service needs to be safeguarded by strengthening the main elements of the whole service. The data service is however no longer defined solely in terms of the work performed in a traditional library and data center. For instance, the information broker phenomenon has been developing a pace in the last two decades, particularly in the USA and other developed countries. There are several brokerage companies operating in the United States itself, the main ones being Information Store and Information Unlimited.

1.2.9. Information Broker

The data broker is a person or company that, on request, tries to answer questions using all accessible sources and is working for profit. The broker has a business approach and utilizes a range of sources, including libraries, to receive responses. Brokerages in the USA cost between $20 and $40 per hour. The price range depends on the complexity of the studies and the nature of the data the customer requires instead of the price procedures. The axial principle is: payment for data. This exchange does not take place in the world of libraries, as many libraries are not cost-effective. There is information, but the user is not charged for the costs. There is a significant difference between freely accessible data and free data.

The services provided by private industry brokers include all the services that librarians traditionally offer and more.

- Both brokers and specialist librarians offer services: abstracting, bibliographical review, cataloging, development of the collection, collecting management, present service of sensitization, document submission, indexing, evaluation of data, internet searching, patent searching, etc.

- Broker services only are: briefing or immediate education, repackaging of data, market research / analysis, recruitment of staff, media cutting, translation services and workshops. Information brokers are specialized in quick and effective service delivery.

- These companies mainly staffed with library backgrounds, supply searches, records and documentation for literature.

- No threat to libraries may be posed to such companies. It actually adds to them by meeting requirements and requirements that publicly-supported libraries cannot and must not attempt to provide businesses, professionals and other customers with unique and costly services.

1.2.10. Information Networks and Information Flows

There are usually formal and informal communication channels in all management organizations.

These formal structures are a scheme that controls power and communications flows, links decision makers at various levels to specified channels of data transmission and creates an orderly flow of information and decision-making procedures. The formal structure mainly includes vertical communication throughout the channel transmits data on organizational ideologies, policies, methods, practices, job directives and performance feedback and upward communication offers management with feedback on performance and issues at reduced levels.

The informal structure reflects social interactions within organizations, regardless of the framework identified. Although both ideas do not necessarily exclude one another, sometimes a difference is created between them. In other words, informal communications are usually spontaneous, unregulated and unstructured in comparison to formal flows. While most casual communication is lateral, certain people within one workgroup play a main role in organizational communication, connecting various hierarchical levels or divisions or acting as 'gatekeepers' of information from outside organizational limits that are of strategically important. In organizations, the informal network has a strong and continuous impact. It is particularly visible in moments of organizational pressure and uncertainty in circumstances which generate fear, anxiety and social interaction and in particular in circumstances where formal communication systems do not efficiently keep staff informed about the problems and problems which they experience.

In the analysis of informal networks the organization is regarded as a mutually independent social system made of 'constituents' and 'connections' among those groups. Within a group, communication activity is intense. Certain individuals act as links between silent groups. Since 1960s, there has been involved research into communication networks by T.J. Allen and others. They identified particular informal communicative and informational roles within organizational settings. The 'technological gatekeeper', the 'internal communication star' and the 'external communication star' are some of the concepts that were put forward and discussed by them. These 'stars' are approached by others within the organization for advice on technical matters due to their perceived knowledge and experience. Because of their professional and personal links with significant 'others' outside the organization, 'external communication stars' are regarded as important information sources.

The 'star' in inner and external communication is technological gatekeepers. These people are some of the 'best' in the organization. The exposure of technological gatekeepers to professional literature is significantly greater, more conference attendants and more professional affiliations are involved. They play important informational roles in the context of both basic inadequacies in other data media and the need for interpersonal interactions in the debate of complicated technical issues. Allen's theory was more usually implemented in writing to other organizations about the role of "border crossing people" in the transmission of data. It can be said that communication obstacles evolve between distinct organizations owing to distinct cultures, conceptual frameworks and terms of reference. Transferring data across organizational borders needs a two-step "border crossing" process which will allow appropriate data to be searched from one hand and disseminated on the other. Therefore, the function of "boundary-scope" needs an in-depth knowledge of local program coding schemas and conceptual structures on both sides of the border, an ability to translate data and communication abilities from one 'language' to the other. In the overcoming of communication problems at the borders, "boundary-crossing" people play a crucial role.

1.2.11. Information Manager Network

For many companies, a proven library or data center is presumed to be the focus of information gathering and dissemination. The Library or Information Center has skilled data experts with the help of certain non-professionals. Combined, these people are accountable for managing the library collection and for any responses requested by the customer. A more efficient focal point for corporate data is the network of data managers. This network comprises a group of IT executives, each of which is organizationally connected to the accountability of a data division. This organizational relationship improves the effectiveness and value of this idea. This idea of the network is indeed like the' technology gatekeeper' in structure and operates. The effort to use a framework for the network is obviously based on the conviction that the fundamental role is to provide data irrespective of the source. The source may be literature, private contacts within or outside the business, professional documents, meeting notes etc. Data and information alone are, however, not enough. For real contributions to be made, clear, concise communication of outcomes must be published or submitted to the most suitable audience. Information executives must constantly operate to deliver not only their data, but the consequences of its use and, in particular, to decide what their job indicates. They are only then seen as contributors to the process of assessment and decision making and are prepared to put the uncertainties of this full partnership at stake with their clients.

1.2.12. Information Filters

Information filter is a name used to describe a variety of information processes to those who want them. Even if the word is often used in common and technical papers describing apps such as electronic mail, a multimedia distribution system and electronic office records, it is often not apparent whether filtering is different from the procedures involved, including retrieval, routing and removal. This is a fresh idea linked to the personalized provision of data.

Information filter are major mediators between the sources of data and the users. In most cases, both sources of information and users have no reciprocal knowledge which could guide users to find information that is relevant to the immediate or long term needs of users. Filters that are logically placed as "third-party" for interaction between consumers and sources should have the expertise and features to critically study the sources of data and forward the data to individual customers as they deem applicable. The unique characteristic of data filters is the ability to function on behalf of both consumers and sources. In the first instance, the most common of which is the "information flood" today, filters help users find relevant information and overcome it.

At the moment, many of the research issues involved in the right design of high-performance filters appear to be dealt with only by a specific and relatively small group of sources and users. This is due to the fact that general purpose alternatives to information filtering demands are extremely hard to provide. User demands appear in general to be wrong exhibiting, and sources of data do not seem to provide sufficiently accurate content descriptions. Due to this double inaccuracy, data filters for a particular context, category of consumers and particular sources are optimized. Filtering data is a fresh form of data service that involves manual and automatic methods.

1.2.13 Knowledge Mediators

As part of the data chain, libraries serve as a link between sources of knowledge and consumers. Owen and Wiercx proposed in 1996 to be understood or appointed as mediators of information. Known as knowledge mediation, the process's through which libraries provide consumers with an insight into current knowledge and help them acquire resources that refer to or contain such information. Knowledge mediators are called institutions or individuals engaged in such processes.

1.3. LAWS OF LIBRARY SCIENCE

The dad of bibliography is Shiyali Ramamrita Ranganathan. He thought, however, that there could be no doubt that the administration of the library is based upon the current needs and understanding of certain vital values. These principles were explained further in a methodical way and limited to five cardinal values. The needed implication and inevitable coincides of the five legislation he established all of these regulations on library organization and management.

There are five library regulations, Dr. S. R. Ranganathan says. The declaration containing these legislation was made, that is to say, in 1928 the law took final form and in 1931 Bombay Asia Publishing House released a comprehensive account of them and their implications.

Basically these laws are:

(a)   Books for use are available.

(b)   Each reader's own book (for all books).

(c)   The reader of each book.

(d)   Save the reader's time.

(e)   Bookseller is a growing organism.

1.3.1. Need of the Laws of Library and Information Science

In the past, there was no evidence for a library as a whole before the wording of bibliography legislation. It looked like prospects were changing completely. Ranganathan thought the legislation of the library to be:

(a) Give Pressure at the Subconscious Level to Work : Scientific methods have been found to be used in natural and social sciences. It is the status of the hypotheses in the natural sciences and the normative of social sciences which are the fundamental distinction.

(b) Helps Library Science to Become an Independent Subject : A topic is thought to be unable to stand in his place without certain basic legislation. Thus, Ranganathan proposes the legislation and places the first step towards this.

(c) Denote Library Practices : In this context the

library practices and practices of the past and the present and which will evolve in the future.

(d) **Serve as a Higher Court :** These regulations are discovered to be relevant to every issue in the fields of bibliography, library and library science. In the event of dispute between canons, the five regulations of library science are appealed for the resolution of the dispute.

(e) **Boundary Condition :** The benchmark within which the librarian can work is thought to be found in this law.

1.3.3. Variants of Five Laws of LIS

One is the generalization of the conception book emphasizing the word document in latest years, and Ranganathan reformulated the legislation as:

(a)   Documents to be used. Ranganathan describes.

(b)   His / his document is each reader.

(c)   The reader of each document.

(d)   Save the reader's time.

(e)   Library is an increasing body.

The five regulations are recommended by Michael Gorman, as "our unique powers." According to him:

(a)   Bookshops serve mankind.

(b)   Respect all types of communication of information.

(c)   Intelligent use of service improvement technology.

(d)   Free access to information protection.

(e)   Honoring the past and building the future.

As "application of Ranganathan's legislation on the Web," Alireza Noruzi suggested the five rules:

(a)   Utilization of Web resources.

(b)   Each user's web-based resource.

(c)   The user of each internet resource.

(d)   Save the user's time.

(e)   Web referred as growing organism.

1.3.3.1. First Law

The first law describes a basic principle and is based on it all other rules of the bibliography. It is seen, not because of its collection or building, but because of the customer, that a library is fantastic. The librarian's motto must therefore be to obtain method and use document. The claim of this legislation is corrected in order to make the user's physical data carrier available. A contemporary librarian who believes in the first legislation will only be happy if the customer always keeps the shelves empty. The consequences of first law according to Ranganathan are:

(a) Location of the Library : Place is the significant component of the library. The library location should be available to the public and affordable. There should be public libraries where more people can visit one enterprise or another regularly and at the same moment the place should be as noiseless and free of disturbances as possible so that severe studying can take place. There is a central location of the University Library. The factory or factory canteen must be located close to a special library. A school and college library does not rely on the place because distances from different parts are tiny. It would nevertheless be better to have it central.

(b) Library Building and Furniture : It is necessary to plan the composition of the library well. It should be inviting on the outside and appealing inside. The structure should be functional and visual at the same moment. The library location should be functional and provide enough room to fulfill the demands for different reasons. The furniture should be supplied to offer the reader convenience and make the most of the library's resources. Racks in libraries should be intended so as not to keep the books high and o make books easy to access on the top shelves.

(c) Library Working Hours : In light of the readers

'needs, the working hours of the library should be chosen. The first law results in the library being opened without leave for lengthy hours and every day of the year. The customers should find their hours comfortable. Each library user is advised to have a key so that the user can always use the library.

(d) Library Staff : It is assumed to operate with skilled and effective employees to make best use of the library. Each member of the employees in the library should act as a friend, a philosopher and a guide to everyone who uses it. The personnel should think in and obey the user's service philosophy. They should be accessible, well-mannered, useful and ready to understand others 'perspectives'; they should be missionary to serve the customer; they should have friendly ways and professional skills to perform the task of the first legislation.

(e) Book Selection : In perspective of the user's current and potential requirements, books should be chosen and obtained. A periodic weeding out of books should also take place.

(f) Shelf Arrangement : The constructed book shelves should be categorized according to a correct sequence, cataloged and ordered.

(g) Reference Service : The personal service will make more use of the document in the library. From the following you can examine the forces of the first legislation:

In the past books have been noticed as unusual, i.e. because of the non-availability of printers, numerous copies are not accessible. It is shown that it took long time to write a document to write the Mahabharata. Thus, the first law was neglected a good deal in the past. All these obstacles can be overcome in modern periods due to the accessibility of printer technology, photocopying, scanning etc. But this trend has sadly stayed a frequent habit in the subsequent generation of librarians, owing to the fundamental practice of maintaining the records. This should be overcome by the contemporary librarian, and there is an urgent need to strive vigorously to eliminate the first law negligence.

A contemporary librarian who has confidence in the first law was thought to be glad only when his reader constantly vacates his / her shelves. He / she is going to them to not snatch the book, but to distribute the new arrival to them as quickly as possible. The forces of the first law have been noted to be traced:

1.　Open access and non-closed access to the library.

2.　Give the world of books free access.

3.　Installation of libraries in bigger towns to be readily reached from each house within a few minutes.

4.　Delivery of books in their neighborhood to the homes of those who would like them to introduce.

5.　Distribute motor vehicle books for people from door to door.

The above forces of the first law were only supposed to be feasible if the library had sufficient funding and could obtain a free copy of books from distinct sources. Everyone pays in this business globe in line with his or her requirements or needs and there is a doubt that a library and information science exception will occur. The first law is therefore dreadful in the near future. In this reverence, when library legislation helps or library readers are prepared to pay for it in accordance with their requirements, the law, the Books, can be used in all aspects.

Books were held in chains in the 15th and 16th centuries in order for their movement to be confined to the field determined by their chains. Such a chaining was more conducive than the use of books to preserve. The first law on library and information science contradicted this practice.

1.3.3.2. Second Law

The second law says that every reader believes his book to be books for everyone. In this, each library reader should have his or her books. It recommends that every reader should be obliged to provide library facilities according to their requirements. It promotes the universal and democratization of the library service, i.e. documents for all, including bad people, sick people, people in prison, neo-literates, ancient men and women, are not just for academics. The papers should be easily accessible regardless of occupational lines and earnings, regardless of ordinary and abnormal conditions, or regardless of an adult or baby. Ranganathan then examines the consequences of the second law as follows:

(a) Obligation of the State

(i) Library Legislation : It has been discovered that it is desirable to consider and not behave as a barrier to the implementation of the second law. This has only been feasible through legislation on libraries that offers funding for public libraries at different rates to obtain free library facilities for everyone.

(ii) Maintenance of a Library System : The public library was thought to have a marginal position in complying with the second legislation with regard to the learners, educators and scientists, since the State is responsible for creating other libraries, including schools, university libraries, universities and special libraries.

(iii) Co-ordination and Resource Sharing : A particular library would not be able to buy records at times. Therefore, according to the second law, the development of a national library network to share funds for inter-library loans in particular.

(b) Obligation of the Library Authority

(i) Choice of Book : According to the second law, every helpful book should be chosen and all unnecessary books discarded. The choice of books should be based on specific requirements. It is the responsibility of the library authority to ensure that a proper policy for the selection and procurement of individual users, i.e. blinds, neo-letters, scholars, children, young people, adults, men and women, etc., is established in a balanced collection in the library. The purchase of a document without a prospective request is a breach of the second law.

(ii) Choice of the Staff : The library agency should, pursuant to second law, select an appropriate and appropriate library team to carefully recruit, subsequently promote, acknowledge and maintain their status as library employees.

(c) Obligation of the Library Staff

(i) Open Access : The library employees were discovered to feel the duty to open access in order to help readers gain access to all books of their own concern. Offering an open access, a reader can approach and manage books directly without any barriers. By open access, a reader can locate the book world and thus have better opportunities to select the correct book.

(ii) Cataloguing : The data contained in a section of a book is often seen to have a reader's interest, but consumers often miss this material. The topic analytical or cross reference entries should be entered to prevent this library.

(iii) Shelf Arrangement : The shelf should be arranged in libraries in accordance with the topic of the paper, not in size or other respects.

(iv) Maintenance : In libraries, maintenance is essential. In the event that libraries are open, there is every chance that the library owner will deliberately or unintentionally misplace some document. To comply with the second law, wrong books must be reinstated. Binding or repairing books should be removed from the racks occasionally.

(v) Reference Service : The referral service is an efficient way of ensuring that the reader has access to the full range of files that the library holds. So the library staff should have proper training in reference work and be able to provide an effective reference service to the user in getting the right book.

(d) Obligation of the Reader

(i) Library Rules Should be Followed : In every library, rules are important. A reader must realize that the rules on libraries are framed in order to maximize library resources and prevent library resources from being used. The rules are intended to increase and not limit the use of the library. The use of the library must therefore be viewed rather as an aid than an obstacle to the inflexible implementation of the rules.

(ii) Maintenance of the System : A good maintenance system should be provided in the library. A user ought to know how to maintain his books. It should not misplace or damage the books in the library. This removes other users; similarly, a user should not injure or remove cards, tear or steal cards from a library catalog, etc.

(iii) Should not ask for Any Undue Special Privileges : The Library is available to an individual, and no one at the expense of others should have any unjustified privileges. There should be no special privileges to deal with current issues, reference books etc. that are so much in demand.

(iv) Returns of Books in Time : The date of issue and date of delivery in the library are important. The issued books must be returned to other users on or before the date on which they are due. If the document or book is unused, the user must return it at the earliest opportunity.

1.3.3.3. *Third Law*

The third legislation states that a reader must find every book in a library. The approach to the document is emphasized in this law. Since this law requires each of the books in a library to find a reader, not one item in the insignificance of the mound should be lost. The following measures should be taken to make this law more effective.

(a) Introducing Open Access : In the event of open access, books in the classified order are arranged in registers and readers have the freedom of access. During their browsing of the readers through the shelves, they may find books of interest which they might not understand. The chances are therefore only improved by the open access system when readers are noticing the books and reading them.

(b) Provision of Popular Department : The popular department, such as the newspaper reading room, the journal section, etc. should be provided which might appeal to the reader and this provision should increase the likelihood that each library will reach its reader. There is an interest of the reader for recent additions, rare books, a specific collection, the festival collection etc.

(c) Book Selection : While selecting a book, attention should be paid so that the chances of books remaining unused are reduced.

(d) Cataloguing : Proper listing of items should be provided. The book may be often disclosed to the reader with cataloging subject, sequence entries, cross reference entries, etc.

(e) Shelf Arrangement : If the shelf arrangement is correct, books can be organized in a wise and intelligent way, so that readers can find books more freely. The library staff should then be attentive to the arrangement by restoring the incorrect books to its proper place and so forth.

(f) Reference Service : Every reader should have a staff that can guide them to take care of their books properly. Each library must provide every reader with personal help if they feel they need it. The reference personnel should serve as a book recruiting agent.

(g) Publicity and Library Extension Service : The staff is believed to be providing shelf guides, bay guides within the library premises, which guide the reader to relevant sites in the library. The referenced people are supposed to make use of publications on the library externally through mass media such as presses, radio, television, speeches, demonstrations, tours, exhibitions, brochure, leaflets, etc.

1.3.3.4. Fourth Law

The fourth law describes the value of the user. The law stipulates that a user must be an active person; therefore his time must be saved. In functional terms, it stipulates that save staff time a reader coming into the library should receive an exact and rapid service. Unrecessary delays can cause distress and unfulfilled readers. Unhappy readers may stop coming to the bookshop. We can see that the fourth law has implications:

(a) Location of library : It was found that the library should be centrally located so that the community served can easily access it.

(b) Open Access : In the proper running of a library, open access plays an important role. The introduction of open access has many advantages. The subjective time decrease, that satisfies readers, is one such advantage of the open access system.

(c) Classification and Cataloguing : The appropriate classification system should be applied to bring together the documents on a given topic and to adopt the related topic.

(d) Shelf Arrangement : Documents would be

arranged according to the degree of mutual relations between subjects to save readers time.

(e) Signage System : To save the time of the reader it should be provided a stackroom guide, bay guides, level guides and gangway guides.

(f) Reference Service : In the fourth law, reference services are required.

(g) Charging System : The method of problem, charge and unload should be performed as quickly as possible.

(h) Centralized Cataloguing : Publishing and cataloging in the press greatly reduces the time factor with the help of the OCLC database.

(i) Information Technology : In order to improve velocity and technology there should be appropriate use of information technology in libraries. IT is signified by the fourth law.

1.3.3.5. *Fifth Law*

Documents, users and personnel are the primary mechanism of the library. In document, reader, user and employees, a library always develops. As a kid develops in every aspect, the development of a fresh library can be contrasted with that of a kid. When a service library has achieved some stability, its development can be contrasted with adult development. In this case, the old document will be replaced by another and the old user will be replaced constantly by new users. The consequences of the fifth law are:

(a) Library Building : In accordance with the fifth law, the construction of the library should be modular and provide for future development.

(b) Choice of Classification and Cataloguing Code: The selected classification and cataloging arrangement should ensure that the growth in the universe of subjects continues at a fast pace.

(c) **Physical Forms of Catalogue :** The physical forms of the selected catalog should be updated, sorted in distinct order, edited, etc.

(d) **Weeding out of Document :** Documents which are outdated and unused should be removed for adequate spacing. This paper should be deposited where it is accessible to be used occasionally or at a key site with library collaboration.

(e) **Modernization, Computerization :** Libraries must be constructed with the recent computer technology and contemporary buildings. Bigger libraries should be computerized so that adequate ordering and maintenance are supported. The documents should be digitized or microfilmed to ensure that the growing collection is taken into account. New purchases should be in electro-journals, e-books, etc. The video terminal and eventually the digital or virtual library should be used to deal with enhanced readership.

The libraries were previously expanded, but today the digital libraries, or virtual libraries or e-libraries do not display the characteristics of a library's volume development. Increasingly advanced techniques are used.

CONCLUSION

In numerous operations in the libraries, the library experts are now using information and communication technology. A bookshop is a service organization designed to promote access to teaching resources, the dissemination of fundamental knowledge, data conservation and dissemination, human culture and civilization. The library roles are used to create the different abilities. The Internet has linked too many pc's and network technology development takes place in time to use the correct reader data. Five laws of library science are shown to be consistent with five brief statements but offer advice and rationale on library and informative practices and teaching. These regulations allow us to derive postulates, cannons and principles that apply in various areas of library and information science. It has been discovered that the first three laws completely emphasize the use by maximum amount of customers of the library records. The fourth law stresses the function of reference librarian and has a huge potential to implement library reforms. It was noted that in the next few years, all legislation will be a source of inspiration and guidance.

REVIEW QUESTIONS

1. Why do you think we need Library Services?
2. Discuss about the disseminations of information in your point of view.
3. What do you think needs more development in the information society?
4. Major advantage of Socio-economic development, according to you.
5. How much do you think role of a library should be in educational development?

2
Library Legislation

Act implies the preparation of the legislative format or format. The Library Act implies in the library context to provide the legal requirement for the establishment under any state or national government of a library scheme, its maintenance, facilities, functions, law and management. The legislation on libraries is capable of governing multiple public library services bodies. It is a tool for the scheduled growth of public libraries to guarantee standardized libraries are established, developed and maintained. It can assist to foster a feeling of self-awareness between the individuals who feel that using library facilities is mandatory on their part.

In 1850 Great Britain adopted the first library act. Most nations currently indicate that public library facilities are free to use.

2.1. NEED AND ESSENTIAL FEATURES' LIBRARY LEGISLATION IN INDIA

Public library services are a natural corollary to the manner of democracy. For safeguarding a free society and a creative culture, free communication is crucial. A public library expects its users to use services only and not money. Where does the funding come from in this scenario? It has come to pass that only legislation can efficiently offer a public library service. Library law is necessary because:

• Legislation enables to create the required circumstances for the establishment of government libraries nationwide.

• The public library should be placed on a sound and safe basis through a library tax levy.

• Making public library independent and saving it from political impact from donation, political gift or personal gifts.

• A continuous, consistent, effective, balanced and coordinated library service and a correct development line for a good administration.

• In order to fix problems of land, construction, legacy, etc.

• For central facilities such as procurement, process, etc.

The law on libraries gives the public libraries financial assistance, but the provisions taken in the legislation on libraries are social, political or economic. There are primarily two methods to provide public libraries with financing through library law. They are

- State's annual budget assignment with capital grants from the central government out of its full resources.
- Using a corresponding grant from the government to levy library process.

2.1.1. Components of Library Legislation:

The following elements of the public library act were acknowledged by Dr. S. R. Ranganathan.

(a) Preliminaries : This part of the Library Act contains a description of the terms used in the Act and the short title of the act.

(b) Top Management : It addresses the questions of library leadership, such as who will handle libraries, which fall within the authority of the Act. It is the second element to be taken into account.

(c) Library Committee : A commission should be set up to provide proposals to the library authority (top administration) and librarians. The library law should make clear who is going to be the members, which functions, rights, skills, duties of such library boards, etc.

(d) Finance : The Act must be clearly state the

- Library process Rate / Local additional or additional fees.
- Goods on which tax is imposed
- The method for obtaining the process from the public, such as car, land, house, other property, etc.
- Process checking of the cash obtained.
- Additional financial sources.
- The library Act itself should include a component in order to keep all accounts and audits every now and then. The Act should also mention the appointment of employees, personnel categories, pay scale, service status and work period.
- The Act should include regulation, rules by law.

2.1.2. Characteristics of Library Legislation

Some of the major features of library law are

- Library law must be straightforward and general. Future changes or developments should also be possible.
- It needs to be free of political impact or modifications.
- They must identify the local, state and national administrations 'corresponding duties.
- It has be mandatory service and free library to everyone.
- The conditions for libraries to thrive should be created.
- In order to have free access to data and knowledge, it must co-ordinate and regulates the library operations in complete recognition of the individuals.
- It needs to satisfy the reader's interest.
- The distinct kinds of libraries, depending on their expertise, can be allocated distinct duties to guarantee better service for the society at the least price.
- Other library kinds must also be taken into consideration

2.1.3. Advantages of Library Legislation:

Following are the advantages of Library Act provide:

(i) Contributes to setting up an organization of public library network.

(ii) A sound management set-up.

(iii) Reliable and ongoing financial aid.

(iv) Coordination of public library leadership and governance.

(v) Central services that can be conveniently offered such as purchasing, processing, bibliographical and other facilities.

(vi)   Possibility, with skilled hands, free of charge, to offer quality library service.

2.1.4. Functions of library legislation

The Government of India's Consultative Committee for Libraries (1958) has suggested the following five tasks of the library law:

(i)   The government's accountability with regard to public libraries should be obviously defined.

(ii)   Legislation should establish domestic, state and district constitutions and functions of the library authority.

(iii) Law should be a guaranteed foundation for the financing of libraries. In two respects, library financing can be established:

- The special library process, and
- Certain educational budgetary percentages are reserved.

(iv)   In the works of the public libraries at all levels, legislation should provide for government representatives' involvement.

2.1.5. Role of Different Bodies in the Process of Enacting Library Legislation

The levying of the library process should not be a requirement when implementing the library legislation. Otherwise, the public or other members of society will lose their assistance. In the process of promulgating the library legislation in the respective countries, distinct bodies can play the following roles.

(a) Library Association : Both local and state library associations and national libraries may establish a strategy for government legislation. You can spread the concept of library legislation using multiple media and platforms. Members of the assembly should be approached and a powerful case for library legislation submitted, particularly by the ministers involved. Legislation of the Indian Library shall provide all necessary assistance and guidance.

(b) Library Professionals : Both the general public and the elite should be conscious of the important role of the library by the library's experts. First of all, you should use your facilities in the organization in which you work and then magazines, radio, TV, etc.

(c) Elite Groups : The elite are responsible for the structure of policies, processes, etc. They are also responsible for providing individuals with the best they can as a leader in society. In view of the role of the library they should take on the function of awakening the public with regard to library services, equipment, etc.

(d) Political Leader and General Public : In the implementation of library law, unique attention is provided to leaders who matter in decision making. The public should also exert pressure to implement the legislation on libraries.

2.1.6. Library Legislation in India

In ancient India, Brahmin was concerned about learning and the common person had to rely on the spoken words of Gurus for his enlightenment. This oral teaching tradition was also used to by general individuals, and therefore no tradition of government bibliographic legislation existed in the ancient India.

(a) Before Independence : Pre independence India demonstrates some important measures to implement the laws on libraries that can be summarized as follows.

(i)   *The Press and Registration of Books Act (1867)* : In 1867 for British India, the Press and Registration Act was approved. This Act was designed to regulate prints and newspapers for the conservation and registration of copies of books and newspapers printed in India. It has assisted certain libraries to obtain free copies of books and retain an ongoing catalog of early printed books in the nation. In this Act, a copy of the book or newspaper was to be sent to the Secretary of State of India, another copy to the Governor-General in Council and a further cup to the local government by the publisher or printer of each book or paper.

(ii)   Funds for the encouragement of literature (1898);

(iii) Imperial Library Act (1902);

(iv)   Model Library Act (1930).

(b) After Independence

(i)   *In the post-independence period, the main steps in implementation of the library laws are* : Imperial Library Act (1948): In 1948, the Indian government enacted the Imperial Library Act. This became the National Library (of India) of the Imperial Libraries of Calcutta (Kolkata).

(ii) *Delivery of Books (Public Libraries Act) 1954* : The Delivery of Books and Newspapers Law was enacted by the Indian parliament in 1954, further modified to include serials in the Delivery of books and newspapers (public libraries).

(iii) *Model Library Act / Bill (1963)* : The Committee chaired by Dr. D. M. Sen also drafted a library proposal in 1963. Then the model library act in 1930 was revised in 1972. In 1966, the library law subcommittee of the Planning Commission produced another model bill for public libraries.

(c) Present Status of Library Legislation in India

In 1945 Kolhapur, princely state of present-day Maharashtra was credited for the first time in India with the adoption of a library law. The act is not functional at present. Nineteen countries in India have adopted laws on libraries so far and the remainder provides library facilities without laws. The following is the list of the nineteen acts

1. Andhra Pradesh (Hyderabad) Public Libraries Act, 1960;
2. Arunachal Pradesh Public Libraries Act, 2009;
3. Bihar Public Libraries Act, 2007;
4. Chattisgarh Public Libraries Act, 2007;
5. Goa Public Libraries Act, 1993;
6. Gujarat Public Libraries Act, 2001;
7. Haryana Public Libraries Act, 1989;
8. Karnataka (Mysore) Public Libraries Act, 1965;
9. Kerala Public Libraries Act, 1989;
10. Maharashtra Public Libraries Act, 1967;
11. Manipur Public Libraries Act, 1988;
12. Mizoram Public Libraries Act, 1993;
13. Orissa Public Libraries Act, 2001;
14. Pondichery Public Libraries Act, 2007;
15. Rajasthan Public Libraries Act, 2006;
16. Tamil Nadu (Madras) Public Libraries Act, 1948;
17. Uttar Pradesh Public Libraries Act, 2005;
18. Uttarakhand (Uttaranchal) Public Libraries Act, 2005 and
19. West Bengal Public Libraries Act, 1979.

2.2. MODEL PUBLIC LIBRARIES ACT AND ITS FEATURES

2.2.1. Model public libraries act of Dr. S. R. Ranganathan

Any discussion on library law in India cannot be finished without mention of Dr. S. R. Ranganathan, pioneering personality. The Model State Library Act, prepared by Dr. S. R. Ranganathan, was adopted at the First Asia Education Conference in December 1930. In 1957 and again in 1972 the law was amended. Here we shall consider the Model Act in its final form (1972).

The Act contained obligatory clauses such as the library rate, the library grant and the termination of local authorities' libraries. Dr. Ranganathan's Model Act has primary characteristics:

(i) The State Library Authority shall be the Minister of Education. It stipulates the obligation of the National Library Authority.

(ii) The authority of State library appoints the State librarian. He will be Chief Executive Officer and also the Chief Executive Officer of library staff. The State Librarian's duties are also specified.

(iii) A State Library Advisory Type Committee shall recommend the State Library Authority.

(iv) For each district and for every city, there shall be local library authorities. The authorities in the local library are corporate bodies. The structure of the Local Library Authority, its formation, function, power, duties of Chairman and Vice-Chairman etc. are vividly stated.

(v) The Library Committees and Service Stations of Branch Libraries are supplied. These committees are of a consultative nature.

(vi) The Library Development Plan Act prepared for the entire round development of library services in towns and districts by the local Library Authority was adopted.

(vii) The Department of Public Libraries is provided with the head of the State Librarian. In addition, the establishment of the State Library Service is labeled by the Model Act. The Act has clearly described a scheme for the State Central Library.

(viii) The Model Act contains provisions on library rules, standards, reports, offenses and penalties, obligatory library cessation of local library authority, mandatory government, grants and state library funding.

Well, yes. We go into the Ranganathan Model Act in detail, and there are the following points:

The Model Act provides for a powerful tool to create a state-owned public library system. The need for a Model Law can be discussed in brief in this context. Each State is not anticipated to embrace the model Act; or rather it is not desirable. However, it is anticipated very much that all States will comply with the Model Act and will also be motivated by its corresponding government library legislation. Indeed, Ranganathan developed the Model Act with this expectation.

In this Act, a "library system" for the State was attempted. Minister Ranganathan's long-term advocacy as the state library authority is the main factor in a state library laws.

In his opinion, the Minister is directly accountable to the parliament and thus to the individuals for the proper enforcement of laws, which is why the National Library Authority is to be appointed in the Library Act.

The State Library Authority's obligation is quadrupled. Item:

(i)   Provision of appropriate State-based library services;

(ii)   Progressive development of bodies for this purpose;

(iii)   Ensuring that domestic policies are implemented effectively to provide the public in every town with appropriate library services.

In the State Library Authority and State Library Committee decisions Ranganathan decides for selecting the State Librarian as Chief Implementing Officer. He is also the CEO responsible for the administration of the State Library Service and workers ' circumstances and all the variables relating to the establishment of the State Library System.

A State Library Committee shall be established to advise the State Library Authority. The chairman of the State Library Committee was appointed Minister in charge of Library Services. The Minister's simultaneous role as

State Library Authority and Chairman of the State Library Committee criticized the specialists of the library.

There is sufficient option for the fail to include the librarian category other than the State librarian in the system of the State Library Committee. In the law, it appears that the role of M.L.A.s or M.L.C.s and persons from the universities should have been explained by the Act. Because it is not known that the primary purpose, unless their roles as Members of the S.L.C. are described, is to pursue the government-built public library system's interest in educational organizations.

The Model Law provides the State Librarian as head in a separate department. To prevent the predominance of the bureaucratic evils over the profession and library service, Ranganathan did this. But there is a potential for a disturbance between bureaucracy and profession in this process which, in turn, can have a major impact on bureaucracy.

The establishment of the "State Library Service" is a key element of the Model Act.

No depiction of the Librarian of the helped Libraries in the City or District is present in the building of the local library authority. Furthermore, the roles of employees from various categories were not described.

The Act includes a consultative library committee for each branch library and each traveling library service station.

In addition, there is the Branch Library Committee on the Branch Library and Village Library Committee on the Traveling Library service station.

In the modern act a significant place has been taken by 'Library Development Plan'. Local library authorities prepare plans, and the state librarian issues the order from the local librarian after the upward hierarchy has been passed through. The Order is implemented by the local library authority. Ranganathan Model Act stipulates

(a)   City Library,

(b)   City Branch Library,

(c)   City Travelling Library,

(d)   City Service Station,

(e)   District Library,

(f)   District Branch Library,

(g)   District Travelling Library.

The Model Act clearly described a State Central Library System. The system consists of

- State Service Library,
- State Branch Service Library,
- State Copyright Library,
- State Library for the Blind,
- State Bureau of Inter-Library Loan,
- State Bibliographical Bureau,
- State Bureau of Technical Service.

The Bureau has jurisdictions specified. Any library or other organization may optionally join the Bureau systems.

The Model Act also regulates the use of libraries', standards and reports.

There is also a significant place in the Model Act of the "reports" prepared by the various authorities, which are eventually consolidated into the annual report prepared by the State librarian.

Compulsory library grant is provided by Act at the stipulated rate and mandatory Govt. The Act provides for the establishment of the municipal and district library funds. The State Library Fund provisions are also provided for in the State Gov. Act. The law also applies. Grant, central government. State government. Gifts and Grant.

The Act, which might have occurred during the execution of the Act, provides for the addition of the necessary segments. The grants also criticized the Model Act. A cautious observance however shows that the Model Act has attempted to create a State-wide system of public libraries that is linked to comparable schemes of other States and to some degree with inter-national systems.

A clear showing of the Public Library Network, its link to the national library system, the academic libraries, and special libraries appears to be missing from the Model Act. However, the Law under Article 4 attempts to establish a public library system within and related to comparable schemes in other States. Another significant and remarkable characteristic of the Model Act is the formation of the Local Library Authority Library Development Plan. This has been very scientifically demonstrated.

2.2.2. Model public libraries bill, 1963 of the govt. of India

The Gov., of India, was the Committee of Drafting the Model Library Bills for the State on the advice of the Advisory Committee for Libraries appointed by the Govt, India (which made a report in 1958), and at the request of the Indian Library Association and other Associations. The above mentioned Advisory Committee is commonly referred to as K.P. In 1963 the Bill had been presented by Gov., India, to President P. Sinha Committee Report and the Committee for Drafting the Model Library Bill.

The following significant characteristics are included in the government library model Bill:

- The State Library Board as Advisory Council on the growth in the State of Library Services for Gov. Advisory Committee.
- Nomination of the Directorate of the State Library.
- The treatment of staff, of the governmental system of libraries, of staff.
- Gov. Fund allocation.
- Library Cess is mentioned in a Bill and no reference

is made to the provisions of a legal deposit of books and journals.

Here are noted several significant characteristics and lacunae of this Act:

The preamble did not emphasize the establishment of a system of public library as the primary aim of the Act.

Here are, a precise Definition of Public Library.

The main tool of the Public Library System, namely that book is well defined in the Act. This Act emphasizes Departments, establishment by the State Government of the organization and links between public libraries and other cultural organizations. No' assisted libraries' are provided under the Act, however the Act seeks to sponsor other libraries and organizations.

There are different categories of representatives of the State Library Authority, but they have not defined their corresponding responsibilities. The S.L.A is not a corporate entity. It is strictly consultative in nature. The Act provides for the establishment of the Permanent Advisory Committee and the Adhoc Committee from the S.L.A.

The Act provides for a distinct Directorate and Director as Head of the Board and as Secretary of S.L.A. The State Librarian shall look out for the National Central Library and advise the S.L.A. in all technical matters. Semi-professional librarians shall organize, lead and oversee them. In the Act the State Librarian should be subject to the Director. It is indicated obviously. The Ranganathan Model Act is in sharp contradiction. The Director is the Chief Officer for the maintenance, control and implementation of the Public Library System Decision.

Clearly indicated in the Act are matters pertaining to the State Central Library. The Public Library Network is not mentioned.

More prominently, the District Library System is articulated in the Act. District Library functions were indicated. In addition to maintaining and providing a district library facilities, efforts have been created to link the Block Library to the District Library and various organisations, particularly the Social Education Institution and the District Library. District Library Committee functions, as stipulated in the Act; also provide the District Library Committee with authority and control of District Libraries and other District Libraries. However, there is no effort in the Act to create a service network. In addition, City and Town Libraries, Block Libraries, Anchal / Panchayat Libraries have not been stated their tasks.

Provisions of City and Town Library Committee, Block Library Committee, Anchal / Panchayat Library Committee are there in the Act.

The Act provides for the establishment of the State Library Fund and the District Library Fund. The collection of' Library Cess' shall be gathered and credited to the District Library Fund, which is to be collected by local authorities of the District. The District Library Committee has two significant duties. They are:

(i)   The District Library Fund is operated and another is

(ii)   To For the District Library employ staffs. The relevant provision is that, if the matter occurs whether or not it falls within district or any other Library Committee, the judgment of S.L.A shall become final.

The controlling officer in the District Library System was appointed No Gov., an officer. The choices of the State Authority were probably left to it. This Act provides for the establishment of Rules by the Gov. and the Director.

The conflict between the Gov. and the State Library Authority (S.L.A., which is simply an advisory body) in regarding of the implementation of decision or powers is one of the possible instances of conflict in the Act.

Similarly there might occur a problem ove: the making of various decisions among the District Library Committee (DLC) and the State Govt, or between the District Library Committee and the State Library Authority etc. In this Act, no specific reference is made to the fields of influence of L.L.A. over the D.L.C. or the Govt and the S.L.A. and D.L.C. regarding the growth of the district library development scheme, which is obviously laid down in the Act of Ranganathan model.

2.2.3. Model public libraries bill, 1965 of the planning commission

The key characteristics of the Model Public Libraries Bill of 1965 (other than prevalent characteristics) of the Planning Commission are set forth below:

(a)   Establishment of the Expert Committee to Frame Library Standards.

(b)   Public Library System Establishment.

(c)   State framework creation for the system staff.

(d)   Cess is not provided for. The Gov. maintains in the State the system of public libraries.

(e)   Preparing the State Library Council's Perspective Plan.

The Planning Commission of Gov., of India, established "Group of libraries working" to advise library growth under a Fourth Five Year Plan. The Act is included in the Report. In the Preamble to the Act, there was no mention of the Public Library, the System. It is indicated obviously in the Law that the government' is to create an integrated and sufficient state library service, sustain it and build it.' The Act is essential in designating a committee of specialists to prescribe service standards at various levels and to suggest the measures required to guarantee the maintenance of this prescribed standard. The State Library Council is provided for by this Act, with the Minister responsible for education as the President of the Library and as the Secretary Director of the State Library. The Council's nature is solely consultative. This Act on the issue of books published by State Gov. is not specifically mentioned State Legislative Assembly and Departments.

The departments a State Central Library should have are not obviously stated. Also, this Act did not obviously contemplate the position of State Central Library as the apex body of the library system in the State. The District Library System was provided for in the Act, and efforts to make the role of District Library prominent at the apex of the District Library System were made. It is very strange to note that the District Library Board is not specifically responsible for managing and monitoring the District Library system. The Act states cautiously the establishment by the State Government, on the advice of the Council of the State Library and State Library employees.

The statement of a perspectives plan to cover the whole State for a period of 25 years, not more than that set period, with a government library scheme is an significant characteristic of this Act. "The Government of the state shall establish within the wide framework job of the plan the annual budgets of the Library Directorate and the Public Library System of that State." For various kinds of library funds, such as State Library Fund, District Library Fund and others, no mention is made. No Library Cess provision is available. The public library service spending was declared to be met from the exchequer. There are no provisions for any committee's borrowing authority. The State Govt shall provide for the establishment of Rules for the Act and the subject matter that may need to be included in the Rules shall also be mentioned.

As mentioned earlier, the Working Group regarded it better to leave the subject of Library Cess on the Government, because the imposition of Library Cess differs considerably. The working group also suggested that the government, India generously share the country's economic burden and that annual government library expenditures should not be less than 1.5% of the annual educational costs. The characteristic features of the Model Act drawn up by the Planning Commission above are the differences between the Model Act drafted in 1963 by the Government of India. The other characteristics of the Planning Commission Act are the same as in Article 2 of this Chapter the 1963 Act of Government of India.

Closer observations indicate that there is no compulsory provision for the model acts prepared by the Central Government. Rather, they left the state governments with those provisions. They tried to establish a library system, but there is no provision for a network of library services in the State central library.

Since independence Government has taken several steps in the direction of the establishment in States of the library system. The Central Government launched a remarkable effort during the First Five Year Plan (1951-56) through the adoption of a schema for the establishment of State Central Library and District Library. An integrated library service pilot project has been initiated. Library service has been linked to the Community Development Project at the time. At that time, however, no attempt by the Union Government to launch library legislation in the States was to do so was made.

Three objectives were underlined in the library development program of the Second Five Year Plan. First of all, state and district libraries are established. Secondly, library law and thirdly the establishment of a public library services network by linking the district libraries downward with village libraries, upwards in the hierarchy with the State Central library and the National library. For the Second Plan period, in 1957, the Education Ministry of the Government India, led by Shri K P. Sinha, then

Director of the Public Instruction of Bihar, appointed a Consultative Committee for Librarians.

The Sinha Committee evaluated Library Services ' current situation in India and suggested a scheme in countries based on library law. Then statutory scheme was examined in Madras and non-statutory systems in various States. The committee has established a scheme that would be appropriate for States, emphasizing the position of the public libraries in society. The report of the Sinha Committee proposes services and Library Structure or Pattern for India. The suggestions contained in this Chapter are in reality elements of Public Library Law and they can be readily taken for recommendation by the Library Law Committee.

These elements are briefly stated :

(a)   Every citizen of India must receive a free library service. Social Services and Libraries with Separate Directorate.

(b)   Specify important departmental functions of the State Library. The Chief Technical Adviser of the library department will be the State Librarian.

(c)   Two chambers will be provided for the State Library, i.e. the State Central Library and the State Lending Library. The State Central Library was ordered to perform certain duties and the State Lending Library has to provide people and district libraries with books and other material.

(d)   Separate Children section in each big library. Separate recommending for children's library service works to be undertaken by the State Library.

(e)   State Library Council to advise the public library of all issues.

(f)   District Library System based on metropolitan centers responsible for their rural regions. Two branches, namely the District Central Library and the District lending Library are expected from the

District Headquarters Library.

(g)   County Library Service Board for the entire County Library Service. District Library Representation at the District Development Board.

(h)   It was highly suggested that the District Library should take up a key position in the district.

While the report of the Committee of Sinha does not define a model act for the States, it can be readily said that the report defines the elements of library legislation, and seeks to advise the public library service network with manifestation of its social entity. It was also suggested that the Public Library Service in the State be connected by a central advisory body to the National Library System and the primary control of the State scheme.

2.2.4. Model state public libraries act of Dr. V. Venkatappaiah

A National seminar on the Model Public Libraries Act was conducted by the Indian Library Association, in cooperation with the Raja Rammohan Roy Library Foundation, in 1990. Dr. V. Venkatappaiah submitted a model bill for public libraries at this seminar. The project was very much appreciated.

The following are the main characteristics of the bill

•   The Head of the State Library Authority shall be the Constitution of the State Library, which shall be the corporate organ and the Minister of Libraries.

•   The State Library Council shall be a consultative body. It is an elect member to be the Chairman of the Council.

•   With a competent director, separate Public Libraries Department.

•   The chain of links between academic and public libraries from village-level up to the state levels.

- Elections from among non-official members of the President and Vice-Chair of the City / District Library Authorities (LA).

- Member secretaries of the City Library and the District Library of City Public Library and District Public Library, respectively.

- Public Library Advisory Committees at every level.

- Systematical release, as is the case with aid universities and colleges, of subsidized libraries.

Venkatapaiah Model Library Law is very detailed, covering almost all elements of the public library system in all aspects. The status of experts has been dignified. It is a very specific definition component. Like the Model Law of Ranganathan, he has given the minister the sole power to carry out the Law. The Minister shall, in addition to other tasks, create Rules under this Act, establish infrastructural facilities, establish norms of library services, provide for appropriate safeguard measures to protect the interests of writers, appoint and regulate personnel, etc. Minister of the state library was proclaimed a corporate business. There is also a State Library Council, a mixture of people from top to bottom who are involved in implementing the Act. This is a strictly consultative body of which the chairman is an elected by the Council's unofficial representatives. It should be noted that it is non-professional which do not involve in library work and did not become a board member.

How a State Library Authority can be a corporation in the model Act is not understood. In addition, to some extent the functions of the Public Library Department and the functions of the Authority of the State Library are overlapping. In reality, the functions of a Library Minister (which is the State Library Authority) as set out in the Act are natural to the degree stipulated by the Government in the Business Regulations as provided by our Constitution and in comparison with the Department and the Authority (which is the Minister). The State Library Authority's statement of tasks is seems excessive.

It has been clearly stated the pyramids of the libraries. But part of "Link maintenance" is nearly philosophical. There is no specific statement on the network of the Public Library. The State Central Library functions have been identified. The State Librarian's importance is right. But there has not been a relationship between the Department, libraries and the State Central library as well as the Public Library Director and State Librarian. Also, the link between Regional Libraries and State Libraries was not specifically identified.

The District Librarian and the City Librarian have complete relevance in technical and administrative issues at the district level and on the city level. According to this Model Law the District Librarian and City Librarian should have the capability, in comparison to the bookstores below the District Library status in the specific District, to operate as the administrative and technical head. The City Library and the District Library's functions were specified in the Law. There is a State Planning Board in the preparation of plans and schemes to advise and lead library system. The popular library plan should be presented to the State Planning Board. There is also a State Planning Council to draft and submit a state library plan for examination and integration with the State's overall economic plan.

There has never been any description of the relationship between the State Planning Board and the State Planning Council. Furthermore, there has been no established connection between the National Library Council (which is a consultative body, too) and the State Planning Board or Council. To some extent this model has been unrealistic because too many authorities or bodies have not been described as having their relationships. A very significant characteristic of the Act is the Board of Library Education. Staff Associations are recognized in the Act. It involves the Personnel Welfare Board, whose status was not indicated. Establishing the Block Development Council is another aspect of the Act hardly acceptable to any State government.

As far as adult education is concerned, state librarians have the capacity to supervise activities in relation to the "all-round state" implementation of adult education activities. In their respective areas, the municipal and district librarians were given significant authority and accountability. Indeed, the exercise of such authority by state librarians, regional library and town librarians relies entirely on the strategy adopted by the central government to eliminate illiteracy. Consequently, the administration of this chapter will make the State Librarian, District Librarian or City Librarian head respectively of the state, district or city authority responsible for adult education program-implementing power.

The aim of this report is to offer a guideline on the program and operations for coordination. Like in many sections / chapters, there was also an officer who was suggested not under the rank of Assistant Director. The establishment of the State Library Service is an significant element of the Act. The Act attaches due significance to the provision of recognition of supported libraries. Predictions were taken to allow these libraries to maintain and be incorporated into the State Public Library system, as well as to maintain their own independence. They are included in the growth plans and five-year plans. Government has a significant scope, which can be discussed, and interferes with the administration of those libraries.

The model act attempted to create an optimal "financial and accounting" scheme. There is a provision for Cess collection and a provision for Government, subsidies. Regarded by government, grant and regulations, the State, Central Government and local authorities shall collect the grant. The Cess methods of collection, City / District Library Fund establishment, State Library and all financial and account nitty-gritty have been addressed. It is not evident how the State Library Authority will retain the State Library Fund, i.e. the Minister.

The Model Act shows an excellent scheme of hierarchical inspection methods and indicates all elements of the government's control over library authorities. Members, staff and members of the Council of State Libraries were proclaimed public servants. There is no clear evidence of a public functioning capacity of members of the State Library Council (S.L.C.) or the Local Library Authority, which makes the S.L.C. an advisory body and the Local Library Authority an entity. This Model Act is intended as an optimal act for a State with too many excellent qualities. It actually intends to perform as a solution, which seems almost impossible to achieve. The author intends to integrate in the Penal Code, State and centrals policies, the Government perspective and even modifications in the Constitution all the optimal elements that lead to the development of a Law, whose implementation assumes optimal adjustments in the planning system. No relationships were established between the higher levels that are between the Planning Board and the National Library Board, the Department and the Planning Board or the Department and the State Library Authority.

The Model of Public Libraries Rules was also established by V. Venkatappaiah. Includes these rules

(i) Administrative authorities : These are all elements of the Council of State Libraries and Local Libraries.

(ii) Date and planning : That is, statistics are retained by the Board, the district planning process and the library authorities publish their annual report.

(iii) Development of assets : This means the

establishment of new libraries and the procurement of ancient libraries, assets from local libraries, etc.

(iv) Personnel management : These are rules pertaining to the State Library Service Constitution by the Government, the creation of jobs, control of staff, rules of behavior for staff.

(v) Finance and audit : This includes information of the Fund's maintenance by library authorities, the Fund's payment of an advertisement, and the rules on the Pension Cum Gratuity Fund, preparation of the library authorities ' annual budget.

(vi) Grant-in-aid : This involves rules concerning all elements of library assistance. What "is not financially sound because of the meager Cess library?" Regulations on Library Association Recognition are also included here.

The basic objective of the Rules is undoubtedly ideal and based on the connection between voluntary companies and Government, machinery. Not Government, people were to go after Govt. Laws and rules that may not be feasible in practice.

2.2.5. Model union library act prepared by Dr. S. R. Ranganathan

In 1948, as part of the "Library Development Plan-Thirty Year Program," Dr. S.R. Ranganathan drafted a Model Union Library Act. This effort was the basis of a suggestion on the Central Government request for the establishment of a national central library.

A closer observation shows that the Model Union Library Act is primarily intended to establish the national central library scheme. It has no link with State Library System, except for two or three sub-clauses. In addition, the sub clauses only relate to cooperation. For instance, the State librarian should help to centralize classification, cataloging etc. based on mutual agreement, standardization collaboration, periodic meetings etc. The

National Central Library positions also appear not to be displayed in a National Library Service Network.

2.2.6. National policy

The norm is that the national policy on the library and information system is much needed for the country, was recognized by all those involved connected with the library program and the execution of Govt. Report of the Art and Culture working group established by the Sixth Five Year Plan Planning committee Period argued for a network of libraries from the villages to metropolitan towns at all levels. The paper again provided a number of concepts that could be considered distinct components of national policies as part of a working group on the modernization of library services and computer science. The Working Group, however, did not declare a concrete National Policy.

In 1985, under the chairmanship of Prof. D.P. Chattapadhyay, then president of the Raja Roy Library Foundation, the Cultural Department of India established the National Policy Committee for the Library and Information System (CONPOLIS). CONPOLIS has presented an interim March 1986 report and May 1986 a final report through a decent amount of processes. The report of CONPOLIS indicated very clearly the National Policy. In particular, as mentioned in the CONPOLIS report the National Policy on the System of Public Libraries promotes the legislation of library in the States, and also the government of the Union.

2.2.6.1. National library system

In its several reports, the Government of India stressed its significance in setting up a national library system in the countries with links to state central libraries. The 1976 Indian National Library Act was adopted. However, the National Library of India Act does not retain a mention-worthy clause in relation to the links between the State Library Systems and the national library system. All other National Library System Recommendations casually noted, with a few exceptions, the above-mentioned linkage. The theses section would try to explore the current library laws in greater depth, ancient laws, recommendations for various studies as far as components of library legislation and model acts are concerned.

2.3. THE PRESS AND REGISTRATION ACT

2.3.1. The press and registration of books act, 1867

The British government in India took concrete form in writing books and other information materials, and, with the introduction of printing presses, several books began to appear on almost every aspect of their lives. Insertion of education provided this with a boost, resulting in the provision of many printed materials. Those who wrote publish and print was thinking of organizing a scheme to keep journals recorded. The East India Company was then encouraged to maintain the journals recorded. The officials tried to collect the books and other publications from different printing presses across India. The East India Company's Board of Directors issued an instruction to forward the copies of all significant and stimulating publications published in India to England for deposit at the Indian House library. Such a statement had an effect that was slow. The Royal Asian Society again encouraged the Indian Secretary to repeat the instructions of the late East India Company's Board of Directors and also requested that catalogs of all publications in India are sent to England. There has been a scheme of voluntary publications registrations, but it has failed.

A scheme of mandatory sales of three copies of each job in India was discovered to be essential to the Government. To do this, a bill to regulate printing presses and newspapers has been implemented in the legislation to preserve copies of books and periodicals with news printed in all of India and to register such books and journals with news.

2.3.2. Statement of objects and reasons:

I.   For many years, the authorities have tried to collect books from the different printing presses throughout the nation and other publications.

II.   The late Court of Manager of the East India Company directed the shipment of copies of all major and inspiring publications to England for storage at the Indian House library.

III.   The Secretary of State for India repeated again in the directions of the late Court of Directors, on the urgently request of a Royal Asian community in London, and wished also that catalogs should be sent to England on all work published in India.

IV.   The above instructions referred in particular to the Lower Bengal Province and the local governments of the province were initiated and a book registration scheme for the benefit of publishers was info med of a scheme proposed by Mr Talboys Wheeler of the Home Office, and matured by Mr. Robinson, Bengali translator of the Bengal Governments.

V.   However, this catalog had to be accumulated by the editor, not with the books but with such incomplete and discrete notices and publicity, as he would gather from journals and other such sources, which discovered that the registration systems had been totally broken down in a good extent and, fundamentally, inaccurate and with only three applications.

VI.   It is clearly not a useful idea that catalogs of books that can be supplemented by private and detailed enquiries should be sent to UK substantially.

VII.   However, the incomplete catalog prepared in 1862 included a list of around 1000 and 500 books, all publicized more or less of concern and significance in the last ten or five years. It is known that there has been an extremely large literary activity in the Province of Lower Bengal in recent years at least and there has been no significant rise in literary activity every year.

VIII. The literature of a country is certainly an index of the opinion and status of the people, and a good government needs to have a good index of that kind.

IX. It is also certainly wise in the interest of Europe's history and academics to provide that a full collection of the press journals in this nation as in England should be produced.

X. Authors and publishers should profit from accessing the public at certain well-known locations by catalogs of their work, and in a very restricted way copies of their works themselves.

XI. Voluntary recording systems for journals have been discovered to be unsuccessful and this bill therefore proposes that three copies or comparable work printed in India should be set up for mandatory government sales.

XII. One copy will be sent to England and the remaining two to be kept at places, for instance in the new museum proposed for the careful preservation, after registration of the book.

XIII. The Official Gazette shall publish a list of licensed works every quarter.

XIV. It is not quite obvious that the provisions of the suggested Bill are currently needed in any other province than Lower Bengal, but to the extent that these regulations are sensible, straightforward and, as far as there is confidence that, as in Bengal, a corresponding literary activity will occur, with the spread of education, in other provinces of the Empire.

2.3.3. Act 25 of 1867

The law was passed and the orders of the Act on Books of 1867 (25 of 1867) were included in the statute book. The Indian Short Titles Act, 1897 (14 of 1897) laid down the nomenclature of the Act.

2.3.3.1. List of Amending Acts and Adaptation Orders

A. The Repealing Act, 1870 (14 of 1870).

B. The Press and Registration of Books Act (1867) Amendment Act, 1890 (10 of 1890).

C. The Amending Act, 1891 (12 of 1891).

D. The Indian Short Titles Act, 1897 (14 of 1897).

E. The Indian Copyright Act, 1914 (3 of 1914).

F. The Repealing and Amending Act, 1914 (10 of 1914).

G. The Repealing and Amending Act, 1915 (11 of 1915).

H. The Devolution Act, 1920 (38 of 1920).

I. The Press Law Repeal and Amendment Act, 1922 (14 of 1922).

J. The Repealing and amending Act, 1923 (11 of 1923).

K. The Government of India (Adaptation of Indian Laws) Order, 1937.

L. The Indian Independence (Adaptation of Central Acts and Ordinances) Order, 1948.

M. The Adaptation of Laws Order, 1950.

N. The Repealing and Amending Act, 1950 (35 of 1950).

O. The Part B States (Laws) Act, 1951 (3 of 1951).

P. The Press (Objectionable Matter) Act, 1951 (56 of 1951).

Q. The Press and Registration of books (Amendment) Act, 1955 (55 of 1955).

R. The Press and Registration of books (Amendment) Act, 1960 (26 of 1960).

S. The Press and Registration of books (Amendment) Act, 1965 (16 of 1965.)

T.   The Press and Registration of books (Amendment) Act, 1968 (30 of 1968).

U.   The Press Council Act, 1978 (37 of 1978).

V.   The Delegated Legislation Provisions (Amendment) Act, 1983 (20 of 1983).

2.4. THE DELIVERY OF BOOKS AND NEWSPAPERS (PUBLIC LIBRARIES) ACT

The 1954 Public Library Act covers all of India with the exception of the State of Jammu and Kashmir. The law covers all of India. Under this Act, a copy of the book shall be provided to the National Library in Calcutta by publisher of every book, newspaper or serial at his own expense and a one-copy copy to three other public libraries as specified by the Central government, within thirty days from the date of publishing it. Public Library Act, No. 27, 1954: Amendment Act, 1956: No. 99 of the 1956 Act amending the Public Library Act and thus "The Delivery of Books and Newspapers, 1954" Act, which states:" The Delivery of Books and Newspapers The' Newspapers' insertions contained in the Amending Act of 1956 on the provision of books (Public Libraries) are also included in serials.

(a) Mode of Delivery : A copy of each book published in the territories covered by this Act by the publisher and publisher of each newspaper is delivered to its own expenses, as soon as it is published, by registered mail or by a special messenger, to the librarian of the three public libraries. The National Library of Calcutta (now Kolkata) is eligible to obtain a copy of any publication produced by anyone else in the nation pursuant to the Book and Newspaper (Public Libraries) Act of 1954. Other copies should also be sent to the public library of Connemera, Madras (Chennai), Central Library, City Hall (Bombay) and Public Library of Delhi. The best of its kind should be the copy to be supplied to the Kolkata National Library.

(b) Receipt for Books Delivered : The person who charge a public library (whether a librarian has been named or another name) or any person authorized on its behalf by the manager who receives a copy of a book shall give the publisher receipt in writing, and shall send the receipt to the editor through a registered post And this receipt is a definitive evidence for the duly supplied copy of the book to the public library of which he is a librarian.

(c) Benefit for the Publisher : All major libraries and listed organizations in the English speaking world and beyond procure the Indian National library. The books obtained through the Public Libraries Act 1954, 56 are contained in the INB. The books are not included. Therefore, the International Intellectual Bibliography library offers the publisher or writer with an outstanding and unique chance to make available their publications as widely as possible in India and nearly around the world. Thus, the Public Libraries Act 1954, 56 also provides the publisher or writers with a business benefit.

(d) Penalty : Any editor, who is in violation of any provision of that Act or any rule hereof, shall be liable to punishment for a fine extending to 50 rupees, but "if the violation relates to a book, it shall also be liable for a fine equal to" the value of a book and the court which is liable to make it clear to the book that a fine of its whole or the part done by him

2.5. COPYRIGHT ACT

Many commentators tended to argue that some court sentences affect libraries and colleges more than the judgments would actually warrant a basic difficulty in the present dilemmas regarding copyright. The desire of certain authorities to accept these inaccurate analyzes was another challenge. A better knowledge of copyright could enable libraries and universities to identify possible actions and strategies while also minimizing the hazards associated with legal proceedings.

The universities and study libraries captured in copyright squeeze. Kinko's Copies and Texaco's recent court orders probed the question of whether a fair use test can be carried out by simply copying private studies and classrooms. Extensive techniques and the accessibility of videotape and electronic database copyrighted works raise questions on the application of copyright law at all. Libraries are at the head of these copyright catches, as they deal with everyday issues concerning the protection and optimal access by library resources for the copyright holders. There are also many distinct activities in Universities which raise concerns about copyright.

This study investigates latest copyright law developments that have an impact on study libraries and universities. This study presents a summary of the principles of copyright, which concentrate on copyright property, fair use and reproduction rights in libraries. In addition, a short study of latest instances and legislation with important potential impacts on research libraries, academia's and future issues concerning copyrights which are not included in court choices and legislation is included in the report. Institutions can start their advance planning with regard to these problems and may impact the form of future legislation.

The aim of the study is to educate, provide a quick roadmap on some of the most difficult issues and encourage discussions of efficient approaches and enhanced answers to problems with copyright. The tendency of many observers to claim that court judgments have a higher impact on Universities and the libraries than would indeed warrant choices was one of the basic problems of the last copyright dilemmas. Some college or library officers ' readiness to take these inaccurate analyzes has been another problem. In many cases, the organizations are unfit to confront the threats of dispute. Acceptance of limiting copyright positions is often an advisable way to deal with a challenging question with minimal liability e :posure. Copyright can be better understood by libraries or universities to define action possibilities and strategies they can take under copyright law, while minimizing the hazards associated with legal proceedings.

2.5.1. The Basics of Copyright

Intentionally, Congress created a brief legislation on equal use that does not involve precise parameters–fair use depends on each scenario. Many applications involve new, fair use assessment and are unable to provide easy or dumb answers. The judiciary is not insensitive to scholarly demands, and the Fair Use Statute expressly recognizes the importance of educational use. Section 108 (on reproduction of works by libraries) is not generally considered to be the source of rights for reserve operations; copies of reserve rooms are made in accordance with the law of fair use. It is important to distinguish Sections 108 and 107 for reserve rooms. Section 108 offers for full versions of products only, whereas the statute of fair use specifically allows several versions for school use, although pursuant to the four variables of fair use.

The United States had national copyright laws since 1790, when Congress first applied its constitutional authority to "encourage the advancement of science" by "ensuring writers for restricted time, the exclusive right to their texts". Only Congress is authorized to create such laws, so the federal law is the basis of copyright in this nation. The law was completely amended last time by Congress in 1976. The 1976 Copyright Act provides authors and their assigns exclusive privileges to copy, distribute, and create most of their initial works. It preserves artwork, sculpture, sound recordings, videotapes, movement images, charts, charts, software programs, databases, and a host of other initial creations. Some works are exempt from the protection of copyright.

In specific, U.S. government works are not copyrightable, but there are many controversies over the copyright capacity of government-funded works or works co-authored with one public worker.

2.5.1.1. Fair Use

If copyright were simply a collection of freedoms solely owned by holders, we would need to obtain approval for any use. But the law also gives the public the right to "reasonable use." Fair use is a privilege as well as a cause of misunderstanding. Nearly everyone will disagree with what is "reasonable," and no one has a definite, legally binding "response." Indeed, Congress intentionally developed an unclear fair use law tha does not give precise parameters fair use relies on each case's conditions. The law provides four variables to take into account:

1. The objective of the use, including education for non-profit purposes.

2. The nature of the job under copyright.

3. The copying quantity.

4. The impact of copying the original work on the prospective market or its importance.

Appendix B to this study shows the complete text of "Section 107" on reasonable use.

By applying these variables, Observers usually agree that the majority of brief quotations from published texts in a scholarly job are fair use. Hard judgment calls surround more complicated instances, longer quotations or copies of distinguishing items such as uniform study tools, questionnaires, videotapes, or computer software. There are plenty of possible "reasonable use" instances. Many uses involve a new assessment, and the responses can never be simple or foolish. Some of the most challenging issues apply to the use of copyrighted works at universities and their libraries: various photocopies for school delivery, various or multiple user access to software, use of videotapes or television program recordings, circulation of recordings or software in libraries, and access to unpublished collections of manuscripts.

Courts have also given little instruction on the majority of problems related to fair use. Fair use of equipment for educational reasons is usually the topic of court choices-the expenses of litigation and charges for lawyers are prohibitive. However, judges are not insensitive to scholarly requirements, and the statute for fair use expressly recognizes the significance of instructional uses. However, developments in the law were far from being exclusively in favor of the academy. For instance, judges have held that a teacher may not draft fresh copyrighted music agreements and send copies to a college choir, and an educational television station may not show a protected movie image without authorization. Another tribunal held that without the consent of the copyright owner, the owner of unpublished documents could not present them to learners. On the other side, judges have often permitted more freedoms to use some products fairly to write history or biographies.

2.5.1.2. Library Reproduction Rights

A second source of usage freedoms of particular importance to libraries is "Section 108" of the 1976 Act, which allows libraries to copy items in accordance with comparatively specific norms. Section 108 does not naturally rely on evaluation and interpretation for each request as opposed to the statute of fair use. Instead, much of Section 108's vocabulary can have practical significance for many libraries without recourse to significant internal advice or complex interpretations. Some of the main operations permitted under Section 108 include:

Section 108 (b) : allows reproduction in another library of unpublished works for preservation or security or for deposit.

Section 108 (c) : allows reproductions of published works to replace a copy that has been damaged, deteriorated, lost or stolen, but only if "unused replacement cannot be obtained at a fair price."

Section 108 (d) : allows the reproduction of articles, or collection from contributions, or small portions of larger works for private study, scholarship, or research by a patron.

Section 10 8(e) : allows for the reproduction of whole works for private study, scholarship or research by a patron if "a copy cannot be obtained at a fair price."

Section 108 (f) (1) : exempts libraries and their employees from liability for copying on unsupervised machines made by employers where notifications are posted as appropriate.

There are various additional te chnical requirements in each of these provisions. Therefore, in Appendix B to this report, the full text of Section 108 is reprinted.

Not every activity in every library is covered by Section 108. Its provisions only apply to libraries open to the public or at least open to non-institutionally affiliated researchers. It is likely that most university libraries meet this standard. Section 108's rights also apply only if "reproduction or distribution is carried out without any direct or indirect commercial advantage." However, the legislative history of the 1976 Act indicates that even in libraries run by for-profit institutions, Section 108 can have some application. Also, reproduction rights do not extend to all types of works under copyright. Many of the rights do not apply to "a musical work, a pictorial, graphic or sculptural work, a movie picture or other audiovisual work other than a news-related audiovisual work" (see Section 108(h)).

Section 108 is not generally considered to be the source of reserve operations rights. Reserve room copies are made in accordance with the law of fair use; reserve rooms may be located in libraries, but they serve as an extension of teaching in the classroom. It is important to distinguish Section 108 from Section 107 for reserve rooms. Section 108 provides for single copies of items only, whereas the Fair Use Statute specifically permits several copies for classroom use, although subject to the four Fair Use Factors. Effective reserves often require multiple copies.

There is no doubt that librarians are familiar with the "five-year reports" originally required by Section 108. The U.S. Copyright Office sponsored the studies to report the effects of Section 108 to Congress every five years. In 1983 and 1988, Congress received reports and abolished the requirement for further studies in 1992.

2.5.2. Recent Developments

Libraries and universities should be careful not to read more broadly than necessary either the case of Kinko or the case of Texaco. A careful analysis of these decisions will show that fair use is alive and well, and significant benefits continue to be offered, especially for non-profit educational purposes. While the case of the Kinko renews concerns about copyright on campus, it also leaves considerable room for fair use to survive, especially if the copying is not done for profit. The case also calls into question the reliability as a legally meaningful standard of the Classroom Guidelines.

The Texaco decision is the Copyright Clearance Center's substantial endorsement. If permissions are easily obtained through the CCC, then fair use is of diminished importance in meeting research goal, according to this case. That court decision is both amazing and foreboding, though it is still restricted to fair use in the profit sector.

Recent instances have created an incredibly limited privilege of fair use for unreleased publications. Two innovations can relieve this construction of reasonable use: a judicial ruling of 1991 permitted the fair use of newspapers and correspondence, and both Congress chambers adopted laws seeking to ensure the preservation of fair use for unreleased texts. Libraries must plan for the continuous return to the public domain of unreleased texts, a method that will start on 1 January 2003.

An addition to the Copyright Act specifically permits the circulation of computer software by non-profit libraries, but libraries should be certain to fulfill the notification criteria of the fresh law. In order to acquire copyright protection, no official copyright notice or register is now needed. Consequently, the inability to enroll or use the notification no longer places the job in the public domain, and the restrictions on reproduction proceed to be set by fair use and other customer freedoms.

1. Kinko's and Classroom Photocopying : In April 1991, the New York City Federal District Court held that Kinko's Graphics Corporation had surpassed its freedoms of reasonable use by photocopying "collections" or "lesson boxes" of curriculum texts for use n local schools. The tribunal found that almost every variable in the equation of fair use went against Kinko's. The tribunal was particularly affected by the profit motivation behind the activity of the Kinko; it was not persuaded that the reproduction was for instructional reasons, at least in the fingers of Kinko's.

The situation revived concerns that equal use would come to an end in many universities and colleges. In reality, the tribunal constantly stated that the unique circumstances of this situation contributed to the finding of an breach of privacy: printing was performed for profit; prints were from sections of the comics; prints struggled for prospective revenues of those publications; and the quantity purchased from each novel was significant. Copying other products or otherwise may not constitute an offense.

A strict ban against compilations laid down in the so-called "Classroom Guidelines" on photocopying for school and study requirements was also denied by the tribunal. The instructions were seen by most academics; they set strict term boundaries on printing. These recommendations arose from debates among stakeholders contributing to the enactment of the 1976 Copyright Act and obtained parliamentary approval as a sensible understanding of "minimum" freedoms of fair use. The publishers are used as formal organizational strategy by most research universities. As suggested by the Guidelines, the publishers urged the court to ban all anthologies, but the court declined, preferring to assess the fair use of each item in the photocopied collection.

Thus, while Kinko's situation renews worries about university patents, it also gives considerable space for reasonable use to live, particularly when reproduction is not for gain. The situation also calls into issue the accuracy as a legally significant norm of the Classroom Guidelines. On the other side, the situation finds it apparent that prevalent methods may be susceptible to copyright surveillance at many universities. An educational purpose that is entirely non-profit cannot sanction all purposes.

2. Texaco and Photocopying for Personal Research Use : The second case of the college seems to have been covered by a second situation. In July 1992, the same Federal District Court, though another magistrate, ruled that a Texaco worker infringed a newspaper publisher's privacy when he produced personal versions of papers, quotes, and emails to the editor for his own study reasons only. The financial conditions once again performed an important part in the result. The tribunal was significantly affected by these results: the printing was eventually designed to encourage the business aims of Texaco; the records were of the complete "collections" and not just extracts; and the prints had a damaging impact on the prospective market value of the copyrighted job.

Perhaps the most significant element of the situation is this last stage. The judgment is a substantial approval by the Copyright Clearance Center; the tribunal argued that the comparatively simple accessibility of permissions through the CCC has decreased the range of freedoms of fair use. The CCC has effectively established quarterly licensing contracts with many corporations in latest years, including several in the oil industry. The business gets approval from all journals enrolled with the CCC to photocopy products with one charge. The program of the CCC not only provides proof of the economic value of a publication, but it can also displace fair use, according to the Texaco judgment. If permissions are easily obtained through the CCC, then the significance of fair use is reduced in achieving study goals. That judicial judgment is both amazing and foreboding, even though it is still restricted to fair use in the profit industry.

As in the case of Kinko, it is possible to distinguish the facts in the Texaco decision from the circumstances generally taking place on campus. Copying on campus in specific is usually without a profit motivation, and in the university society, copyright registration programs are not yet well developed. But the situation shows that a tribunal may be prepared to construe as a copyright infringement even personal reproduction for study requirements. The situation is an open invitation to the CCC to expand its program, including research libraries and universities, to more kinds of organizations. Indeed, a pilot program comprising several universities has been finished by the CCC, and further parts of this study discuss it more fully.

Libraries and universities should be careful not to read more widely than necessary either the Kinko case or the Texaco case. Each situation should require a re-examination of photocopying methods, but each instance provides cautious administrators a promising opportunity. In specific, Kinko's seems to suggest that all photocopies in anthologies involve authorization to prevent future liabilities. Similarly, Texaco indicates that personal reproduction of studies is either prohibited or restricted, or that each organization now has to engage in all CCC registration programs. These findings may assist fend off litigation, but they also constitute severe misreading of instances and are detrimental blessings of the rights of fair use that the law still maintains for most research libraries and universities.

ARL's attorneys submitted a more thorough assessment of the Texaco judgment and its impact on the freedoms of equal use and reproduction of libraries. For more data, please respond to this assessment.

3. Fair Use of Unpublished Works : Recent instances concerning writer J.D. from the Second Circuit Court of Appeals. Founder of Salinger and Scientology, L. Ron Hubbard has created an incredibly limited freedom of fair use with regard to unreleased works, especially letters, newspapers, diaries, and other items that are frequently stored in library libraries and used in composing history and biography. These instances do not undermine from the particular freedoms under Section 108 to print written publications. Rather, they have limited rights to cite the written texts from-or even to paraphrase them.

This confining construction of reasonable use may be alleviated by two advances. First, a Second Circuit judgment of 1991 permitted a biographer to reproduce short extracts from Richard Wright's publications and correspondence. Second, both Congress chambers have enacted laws that seek to ensure fair use for unreleased plays to survive. None of these advances is a huge extension of customer freedoms, and a work's unreleased essence can still be a variable limiting fair use.

Libraries retaining collections of manuscripts should be ready for periodic inquiries from customers on their freedoms to cite unreleased texts. Such problems of fair use can be defined in the copyright strategy declar tion of the institution. This law's ambiguity can also be discussed when libraries obtain collections of manuscripts. The donor or vendor may own the copyrights of the collection's products because either the applicant is the author or the author has acquired the privileges. The buying library should regularly pursue ownership of the copyrights and ownership of the products themselves. If the recipient is unable or reluctant to pass the copyright, the library should thoroughly record the title and email of the copyright proprietor and promote the applicant to pursue guidance on the maintenance or management of the copyright and ensure its transparent and timely distribution upon potential purchase or murder of the proprietor. Users of the libraries of manuscripts will probably need to acquire approval from the owner for even popular quotation, and the accessibility of such data in the library will considerably speed up the scientists ' search.

Libraries must also plan for the continuous transfer to the government domain of unreleased publications, which will start on 1 January 2003. The preceding principle was that in perpetuity unpublished texts received copyright protection. Thus, without expiration, even the most prominent people ' journals and correspondence were susceptible to copyright constraints. With the passage of the 1976 Act, Congress abolished that rule and subjected unpublished works to the limitations of all copyrights: the life of the author in general, plus fifty years. The law postpones the implementation of the fresh rule until 2003 instead of immediately assigning decades of endangered publications to the public domain. In that year, the original writers ' texts that disappeared more than fifty years before will be accessible for use without restrictions on copyright. Every year there will be fresh papers published by writers who have resided a year sho. ter. This fresh law will have a major impact on the purchase and use of fresh manuscript papers in just ten years.

4. Library Circulation of Computer Software : In 1990, Congress modified the Copyright Act to ban computer software business loans. The bill says explicitly:

Nothing in this subsection shall apply to a non-profit library lending a computer program if each copy of a computer program lent by that library has attached a copyright warning to the packaging containing the program in accordance with the requirements prescribed by regulation by the Register of Copyrights.

The law was obviously intended to limit software borrowing for profit, but not to eliminate its use in the instructional framework of non-profit. Libraries should study their strategies and procedures to ensure that they comply with the demands of the fresh law and that they are not more rigid than permitted by law.

5. Elimination of the Copyright Notice Requirement : The United States entered the Berne Convention in 1989, a global agreement that provides for the mutual security of copyrights initially guaranteed under the legislation of each country. Thus, in many other nations, a copyright acquired under U.S. law can be protected. Congress revised the U.S. to enter and adhere to Berne. Several aspects of the Copyright Act. The elimination of the obligation to include a copyright notice on copyrighted items was an important shift for libraries and universities. The requirement was relaxed in the original 1976 Act, but now there is no need for the familiar notice of copyright usually the "C" in a circle, name, and year. Since the 1976 Act was passed, registration of the job has also been voluntary.

Users must now suppose that all copyrightable products are in reality covered by copyright without notification or permission being needed. The failure to register or use the notice no longer places the work in the public domain, and the limits of copying are still defined by fair use and other user rights. Moreover, the lack of these formalities may also render it hard to acquire certain data about the plays. For example, when setting the date of a work, catalog librarians often rely on the notice of copyright.

6. Elimination of Eleventh Amendment Immunity for State Institutions : A few judges held in the early 1980s that it was not possible to bring patent proceedings against government colleges. For hundreds of organizations across the nation, the outcome was complete immunity. Not soon lasted this peculiar situation. The Eleventh U.S. Amendment Constitution precludes federal courts from prosecuting countries for financial damage. The Eleventh Amendment's aim is to safeguard state coffers from the federal government's strong power. But federal law also states that it is necessary to file in federal court all violation activities taken under the Copyright Act.

In one noteworthy situation, UCLA was prosecuted by a computer manufacturer declaring breach of copyrighted programs. The federal district court rejected UCLA's complaint; federal court could not hold the state university responsible. That judgment was confirmed by the Court of Appeals and by the United States. The Supreme Court denied hearing the argument. The immunity has been created for UCLA and other state organizations. In previous, insignificant instances, the Supreme Court permitted instances to continue against countries in federal courts if Congress expressed its intention to abrogate the immunity of the Eleventh Amendment in regard of the law in issue. The Copyright Act was revised by Congress in 1990 to create that specific declaration of purpose. State schools ' protection has now disappeared. The same copyright laws now apply to state and personal organizations.

2.5.3. Future Developments

A 1992 report from the Congressional Technology

Assessment Office recommended that librarians and others be involved in the development of computer software guidelines on fair use and library use. Librarians need to take the initiative and accept the challenge. Failure to provide credible advice on fair use of software and other new media has forced manufacturers and consumers alike to increasingly depend on licensing contracts to delineate privileges and responsibilities.

The growing dependence on permit contracts as substitutes for copyright law generates conflicting rules and many occasions contributes to fresh constraints that go beyond the requirement of the law. Fair use and licensing treaties are not just replacements. The "University Pilot Program" conducted by the CCC in 1990 for a proposed annual license was one of the most significant developments in collective licensing, but the anticipated agreement has some deficiencies.

1. Guidelines for Fair Use of Computer Software: For libraries and universities, the fair use of computer software is the unknown of greatest importance. Congress did not in any way restrict the statute of fair use to certain media, but software often does not seem to be relevant to traditional rules of fair use. For example, the amount of work copied is one factor in the fair use analysis, but software is rarely of any use unless it is copied in full. However, many opportunities for reasonable use stay: non-simultaneous use of given software package at more than one place; display of program combinations during teaching meetings; or inverse engineering of safe software. There are countless opportunities for fair use apps, but they are also far from being resolved.

A 1992 report from the Congressional Office of Technology Assessment recommended that librarians and others participate in developing guidelines on fair use and library use of computer software. Librarians must take the initiative and accept that challenge. The failure to act and the failure to identify and preserve user opportunities will leave a vacuum for other interest groups - with potentially contradictory objectives to give shape to understanding this crucial aspect of copyright.

2. Increased Reliance on License Terms : Failure to provide credible advice on reasonable use of technology and other new materials has forced manufacturers and consumers alike to progressively depend on licensing contracts to define freedoms and responsibilities. The outcome is an incoherent implementation of rules and the feasible recognition of constraints that go beyond the demands of the law. There is usually a diversity of contracts or "permits." Sellers often outline contracts in the software trade that are designed to be conditional on buyers. Such contracts often include constraints on the use, copy, lend, or sale of the job. An organization that buys a lot of distinct software bundles from a lot of distinct providers will probably be susceptible to a variety of distinct regulations. Complexity alone may prevent customer property discovery.

Another result of depending on permits is that they often contain new constraints that go beyond the patent rights of the owner. No one can state with assurance whether a person is permitted to perform a program from one laptop to another until potential laws or judicial rulings explain privileges. Fair use rules give a good argument for supporting the legitimacy of carrying the disc. Yet this operation is forbidden by many permits. They should acknowledge that permits are open to negotiation when libraries and universities obtain their holdings. They should study the conditions and critically examine their prospective impact on the achievement of organizational goals. They should also withstand concluding contracts that explicitly or implicitly restrict law-setting freedoms.

In this sense, it is becoming increasingly important to follow creative rules for the reasonable use of technology. Fair use and licensing treaties are not just replacements. Rather, a better perception of possibilities for fair use can be a vital move towards achieving better contracts.

3. Participation in Collective Licensing Arrangements : As mentioned above, the Texaco situation gave the Copyright Clearance Center fresh exposure as a way of acquiring reproduction approval-including reproduction for personal study requirements. Although most focus has concentrated on the CCC, comparable or supplementary programs are offered by other organizations. For example, the National Association of College Stores, the Association of American Publishers, and University Microfilms, among other organizations, have set up systems to grant copyright permissions or provide copies of articles and books with copyright ownership clearance.

The "University Pilot Program" conducted by the CCC in 1990 for a proposed annual license was one of the most significant developments in collective licensing. The study was attended by six colleges and universities, and the CCC collected data on the types and quantities of copied materials for different purposes. A full public report on the study has yet to be published by the CCC and a long-term license agreement has yet to be offered for colleges and universities. But there are certain deficiencies in the expected contract. For example, making "anthologies" for classroom use is not expected; it may not cover copies of reserve rooms; the CCC does not represent all publishers and copyright owners; and the CCC does not define any scope of fair use that does not require permission or fee payment.

Collective management whether through the CCC or another organization-provides schools and colleges many precious advantages. It can speed up the method of approval and provide safety from many prospective allegations for breach. While there is an increasing temptation and momentum to engage, respondents should scrutinize any future "blanket permit" and acknowledge its constraints. The CCC's license in its expected form would not embrace all library or university needs, leaving the institution to continue the burdensome task of defining fair use and seeking individual permissions for a great deal of copying.

2.5.4. Potential Strategies and Options

The goal of an institutional copyright policy should not only be to comply with the latest standards, but also to identify the institution's maximum opportunities to pursue its informational and academic goals legally. Many normal shape strategies are questionable answers to a streamlined law that should tackle various conditions, especially the Classroom Guidelines.

Libraries and universities need to take a leading position in developing problems of copyright as they arise. Many freedoms of fair use are not well defined, and those voids in the law are invites to suggest and discuss rules for various interest groups.

1. Reevaluation of Copyright Policy Statements: Changes in legislation and enhanced patent disputes have encouraged many librarians to check their current positions on copyright strategy. Su h a study should be aimed not only at achieving adherence with the recent norms, but also at identifying the institution's peak possibilities to pursue its informational and educational goals legally. For instance, the instances of Kinko and Texaco send a message of decreasing fair use, but a thorough assessment of those choices will demonstrate that fair use is alive and well, and it remains to deliver important advantages, especially for non-profit instructional reasons.

The increasing difficulty of the legislation also shows that "easy alternatives" are often no answer whatsoever. Many normal shape strategies are questionable answers to a streamlined law that should tackle various conditions, especially the Classroom Guidelines. The American Library

Association provided photocopying an option model strategy in 1982. While it may require a new evaluation, it shows that there are distinct definitions of fair use accessible, and some definitions are best adapted to the goals of the library or university.

2. Coordinating Responses to Copyright Issues : Coordinated efforts will lead in the most significant settlement of copyright problems. Various library employees and university group representatives need to operate together to communicate their requirements and views and develop norms that represent real requirements and gain broad assistance. When formulating policies, librarians need to seek guidance from faculty, administrators, and legal counsel. A commonly recognized collection of norms also requires assistance from outside the community of libraries and universities. When the Technology Assessment Office suggested developing computer rules, it rightly encouraged various organizations to meet including computer manufacturers, teachers, and representatives of the general community. It also suggested the U.S. The method is taken over by the Copyright Office. Any subsequent instructions would undoubtedly be given enormous legitimacy by endorsements from divergent interest groups and the central government agency. In any such trials, librarians and college representatives must be certain to discover or establish a prominent position.

3. Effective Leadership for Emerging Issues : Librarians should not perceive copyright as a strictly external force that directs the institution's range of activities. Copyright is a set of opportunities and the task of the librarian is to identify as many opportunities as possible under the law to meet the needs of scholars and the research community. Copyright is also not only a negative force; the law provides protection for new works created by the library or on campus, and the rights of owners are an incentive to create and distribute many new materials. Libraries and universities, above all, must take a leading role in shaping copyright issues as they emerge. As described earlier regarding computer software, many rights of fair use are not well identified, and those voids in the law are invitations to propose and negotiate guidelines for various interest groups.

CONCLUSION

No country in which library law exists can provide fully satisfactory and effective library services. In spite of the fact that laws have been revised in most countries, they all have problems to some extent. Again, there are many countries without legislation, but in comparison with the countries that have legislation, they serve the general public better. Chapters deal with penalties and proceedings, appeals, Press & Registration of Books Act and Repeal and Savings respectively, all attempts to implement the Press & Registration of Books Act have been adopted in a perfect way.

REVIEW QUESTIONS

1. What are the needs for Library legislation?
2. Describe the advantages and functions of library legislation.
3. Explain the model public library act and its features.
4. Analyze the press and registration act.
5. Explain the copyright act.

3
Documentation And Information Centres

LEARNING OBJECTIVES

After studying this unit, you will be able to:

- List and clarify the goals and objectives of the book and data specialist organizations.
- Explain book organizations' programs and operations in achieving their goals and goals, and
- Identify and outline the operations within and outside India of certain library and data organizations.

3.1. DOCUMENT

A paper is any tool that contains documented academic Endeavour proof. The term document in HANS P LUHAN's words is used "To designate a block of physically confined information in a medium such as a letter, report paper or book. The term may also include the medium itself." According to Oxford English dictionary, "A document is a single piece of written or printed matter that provides evidence or information on any subject matter.

3.2. DOCUMENTATION

The paperwork is document-based or document-dependent. Those who work with data compilation or information of any kind use the term in the wider context. In the limited context, paperwork, as used by scholars, is the quote of published proof in assistance of a declaration, while in the liberal context, paperwork includes all actions linked to files from registration to dissemination. Therefore a quantity of vagueness of significance connected with the word and there is no all agreed connotation.

Usually it was defined in such ambiguous words as, "A method by which all papers of all types of fields of natural operation are carried together, categorized and circulated. It was so recognized by the Paul Otlet, whose" Traite de documentation "is now considered to be a standard debate of the topic.

R.S Ranganathan, India's father of library science, an excellent mathematician describes it as follows: "Documentation is the complicated of procedures engaged in a pin-pointed, exhaustive and expeditious sequence of nascent expert thinking. Bradford describes paperwork as 'the practice of gathering, classifying and easily evaluating documents of all types of academic operations to present the current literature to the artistic expert, carrying the topics of his inquiry so that he may be fully conscious of the pervasive accomplishments of his genius on job already accomplished'. He also says, "Documentation is an art of practical necessity practiced by the fraternity of enthusiastic devotees whose painstaking work contributes to the progress of society in modest obscurity."

Jesse H. Shera described paperwork as' the set of methods needed for organized submission, organization and interaction of registered specific knowledge in attempt to make the data stored as accessible and as helpful as possible.' While, according to Ralph R. Shaw,'

Documentation is any method related to,' detection, processing, organization, processing, retrieval, retrieval, retrieval in more useful forms, synthesis and dissemination of print or other recorded academic content.

The word's most important concept is that established in 1945 by ASL1B for the Journal of Documentation, namely, "Recording, organizing, storing, remembering, converting into more helpful types, synthesizing and disseminating."

3.3. DOCUMENTATION SERVICE

The documentation service includes:

1. Supply of lists of documentation known as service of Current Awareness.

2. Reprographic work i.e. Reproduction of reading material required by a scholar in order to prepare a photographic copy in micro form such as micro fiches, micro cards or microprints, etc.

3. Translation work i.e. important articles are translated into one that is readable by scholars of the particular country from different foreign languages.

4. Preparing on-demand adhoc bibliographies.

5. Abstracting and indexing subject matters papers where other abstracting and indexing services already in existence failed.

6. Preparation of incomplete manuscript catalogs in various areas of Indology topics.

7. Service for information

3.4. SALIENT FEATURES OF DOCUMENTATION

1. The function of gathering, classifying and rendering readable in all types of academic documents.

2. Knowledge documentation and information resources systematically organize such documents in order to find them rapidly and disseminate both

information and information components by multiple methods.

3. Specialized informations, capturing, organization and dissemination.

4. Science in the collection, storage and organization of stored data content or records for optimal retrieval.

5. Selecting, classifying and distributing data.

3.5. DOCUMENTATION AND INFORMATION CENTRE

The Documentation Center has constructed an extensive data compilation since its creation in 1969 to add to the worldwide exchange of information on criminal justice and to help the international community formulate and implement enhanced crime and justice strategies. The Center's operations include collecting, analyzing and disseminating of law, statistical and bibliographic records forming the collections of the library.

The Library contains over 20,000 monographs, 1,250 newspapers and yearbooks, dozens of thousands of UN system papers, other global and regional organizations, domestic institutions and NGOs, multimedia content, grey literature on crime prevention and criminal justice problems.

The Center provides internet links to all of its facilities, such as library catalog and criminological thesaurus, electronic materials, bibliographies, directories, content sheets, full-text journals, abstracts of monographs and personalized alerts tailored to its customers' requirements.

The UNICRI Library is component of a powerful network of UN and UN system libraries sharing knowledge, best practices and assets and working together to guarantee the highest value of products and facilities for their customers.

The Center provides professionals around the world with a tool for developing and implementing technical measures and studies, supporting coaching operations, producing and disseminating UNICRI journals, providing data on the mission of the Institute, range of operations, previous and present programs.

3.6. LIBRARY AND INFORMATION PROFESSION: ETHICS AND STANDARDS

Basic core principles that describe the career task of librarians and data specialists include safeguarding academic liberty, liberty of speech, liberty of entry to knowledge, data and society, and adherence to the concept of ideological, political and cultural independence. Librarians and information professionals should be publicly trusted by people, experts who mediate between writers and consumers of data, and published and data materials that consumers need to conduct multiple duties and achieve their objectives.

The Code of Ethics for Librarians and Information Professionals sets out basic principles that are binding on all professional representatives and identify their social mission and ethical responsibility in all professional environments. These concepts are split into three organizations. The first includes overall importance values. Five subsequent subgroups of the second category include ethical norms that define the profession's obligation toward the public, book and data consumers, school and data assets, the academic society, workers, and organizations. Third band includes commitments related to professional ethics popularization and accordance with its values.

3.6.1. General principles

1.   Librarians and information professionals are employees of the industry that stems from the tradition of the librarian industry, the industry that has its own ethos, framework, organizations, specialist education and training scheme. Librarians

and information professionals recognize tasks arising from the government task trait of librarianship and specialist data facilities and strive to form and reinforce their profession's positive image.

2. The job of librarians and information professionals is to acknowledge, meet and create customers' requirements for data, education, science, culture, esthetics and entertainment. Their specific mission is to create possibilities for open public access to domestic and foreign data assets and to preserve and communicate the social and science legacy to the government.

3. Librarians and information professionals are opposed to censorship and any types of restricting entry to data, knowledge and society, relating to rationality, common sense, and best practice.

4. Libraries and data centers are "government trusted" organizations whose motto in all areas of their operation is "the public welfare". With regard to the tasks and duties of their employing institutions and the use of their collections and information resources, librarians and information professionals are obliged to provide high-quality services with equal diligence to all users.

5. While maintaining the variety of customers, the concept of equal opportunities and regard for human rights, particularly the right to intellectual freedom and open space to knowledge, data and society, always guides librarians and information professionals. They endeavor to know relevant ethical principles for organizations with which they work and collaborate and attempt to honor them.

6. Librarians and information professionals honor the privacy and discretionary rights of consumers.

7. While operating in publicly funded schools and data centers, librarians and data experts attempt to

provide their fundamental data facilities at free of cost, especially access to fully valuable resources of a behavioral, usable or enjoyable type, within their organization, beyond it and in their digital room.

8. The freedoms of author and intellectual property are respected by librarians and information professionals.

9. While paying for the high quality of their facilities, librarians and data specialists are continually perfecting their expertise and abilities and striving to use all their specialist abilities in their career activities.

3.6.2. Librarians and information professionals toward the community

1. Through their job, librarians and information professionals add to the growth of people and the society as a whole.

2. In the society, librarians and information professionals continually disseminate awareness of the significance of knowledge and data as well as free entry to it to enhance the standard of lives, the growth of culture and civilization.

3. With regard to their professional operation, librarians and data specialists never position private concern before the community's concern.

3.6.3. Librarians and information professionals toward the user

1. Regardless of the nature of their work, librarians and information professionals always work for the user's benefit, respect him and endeavor to learn about his needs. Librarians and information professionals assist consumers reach the products they are looking for, irrespective of their material, provider and process of access.

2.   Librarians and information professionals protect and keep secret all user-related information, their interests and personal data, only for the purposes defined by the law. Librarians and information professionals provide consumers with the liberty and privacy to use the funds that are circulated / accessible.

3.   Librarians and information professionals provide customers with the finest research / working circumstances by ensuring high-quality study workspace, easy, understandable and logical organization of gathered and distributed resources, ready data items, responded data inquiries and executed initiatives. Librarians and information professionals are concerned about their organizations ' esthetic and operational importance, suitable type of job, and pleasant atmosphere.

4.   Librarians and information professionals know and honor the reality that not all consumers can receive data and use the library similarly. They strive to equalize such consumers' opportunities, operating with specific concern for the advantage of disabled and culturally poor minorities and promoting social minorities (racial, domestic, religious, etc.). As participants to the system of education for kids and adolescents, librarians and data experts strive to create their data requirements and culture of learning.

5.   Librarians and information professionals are concerned about the high quality of facilities they deliver, striving to satisfy all possible customer satisfaction requirements. Librarians and information professionals provide users with honest information on the full and actual scope of library services, the content of the collections and information resources circulated the quality of the information tools used and the possibilities of

compensating the limits of the services available through the cooperation of libraries and information centers.

6.   Librarians and information professionals strive to provide consumers with straightforward, well-known data about the laws to use the libraries and data centers, avoiding casual alternatives that create hidden rights. Librarians and information professionals are trying to give their facilities to as many customers as feasible, yet they are allowed to deny those who do not conform to established values, breach the laws or render other consumers uneasy as necessary.

7.   Librarians and information professionals stay impartial in all their career operations and prevent any subjective assessment.

8.   Assuming the position of steward to customers, librarians and information professionals treats with regard and accept all criticism raised by consumers. Librarians and information professionals respond to all problems immediately and honestly.

3.6.4. Librarians and information professionals toward library and information resources

1.   All resources assigned to them are respected by librarians and information professionals. Not restricting entry to them, they strive to preserve library and data assets rationally and to protect them. Librarians and information professionals conform to computer hardware and software usage laws, including licensing contracts, as well as the netiquette. They worry about accordance with the resource utilization laws, especially those resulting from the copyright / author freedoms of operation, not enabling the manufacture of illegal translations or modifications of initial products.

2. Librarians and information professionals are striving to guarantee the highest standard of the information systems and facilities they use or generate to the finest of their understanding.

3. Librarians and information professionals adapt to their institution's library and data services to the requirements of the audience and their specialist environment, taking account of their content's suitable norms and ongoing reviews. With regard to resource selection and choice, librarians and information professionals comply with the principle of impartiality, objective and competent evaluation, informing users about accepted resource development rules.

4. Conscious of the variable importance of book and data products, librarians and data specialists are striving to know different techniques of asset assessment, bringing into account the opinions of science and literature reviewers. While choosing and cataloging assets, they are driven by user requirements and the concept of prioritizing the best value products.

5. While procuring, cataloging, arranging, choosing, and distributing book and data materials, librarians and data experts withstand and stay impartial to all forms of discrimination; they strive to use such instruments to catalog records and organize libraries that prevent customers from becoming prejudiced against any specified text or materials.

6. Where certain book products or data resources are removed from publlic consumption because of their rare, valuable, secret or culturally harmful personality, librarians and data experts educate consumers about the presence of such products in a particular organization and government the laws and laws on their use.

3.6.5. Librarians and information professionals toward their colleagues and profession

1. Librarians and information professionals are working reliably, learning the best practices used in librarianship and data facilities, and striving to provide customers with ideal facilities. Librarians and information professionals comply with the hiring institution's standard of practice.

2. Librarians and information professionals strive to become group which independent of artificial structure, power and custom, but in accordance with the values of excellent organization of job. Librarians and information professionals know that their job is a sort of business that needs them to be scrupulous, timely, diplomatic, well-balanced and well-managed. Only those areas of library and data facilities where their expertise and abilities are sufficient are fully engaged by librarians and information professionals.

3. Librarians and information professionals are driven by the well-understood concept of personal solidarity, taking care of their profession's positive image.

4. Respecting and knowing the accomplishments of their colleagues, librarians and data experts use only exclusive statements in the debate-also in conversation with their subordinates and supervisors. Remaining in the professional relationship does not release anyone from compliance with legal and professional ethics standards.

5. Continuously developing their abilities and expertise, librarians and data specialists aim to improve their working environment / community and the performance of facilities provided by their working organizations and assist their colleagues, especially

their subordinates, in developing their working abilities. Librarians and information professionals are supporting their associations and specialist organizations.

6. Librarians and organizational information professionals suppose a distinctive accountability for complying with the rules of competent conduct and ethics by their subordinates, setting their colleagues a strong example individually.

7. Building connections to library and data services instruments and generating data, librarians and data experts concern about the quality, under-standability, communicative importance and accuracy of the material being communicated as well as their own opinions.

3.6.6. Librarians and information professionals toward the employer

1. Librarian and information professional staffs are very loyal. They worry for their hiring institution's excellent reputation, they strive to build and strengthen their institution's favorable government picture.

2. Librarians and information professionals are striving to understand and deepen their knowledge of their employing institution's tasks and objectives and to support them through their own activities.

3. Librarians and information professionals use their knowledge and professional skills to develop their employing institution and improve their methodology, information resources and tools.

4. Librarians and information professionals are entitled to expect, supply and request fair wages that are sufficient to their professional qualifications and job difficulties, although they should never render their job performance conditional on their wages.

5.　Librarians and information professionals prevent any unethical procedures that may be suggested or recommended to them.

3.6.7. Final resolutions

1.　Librarians and information professionals conform with the professional ethics values identified in this Code in all their operations linked to their career.

2.　Librarians and information professionals are striving to deepen and raise consciousness of ethical and legal elements of library data and service activities.

3.　Librarians and information professionals withstand their professional group leaders' unethical behavior.

3.7. PROFESSIONAL ASSOCIATIONS: NATIONAL AND INTERNATIONAL

In the previous systems, you gained a relatively excellent understanding into library historical views, library growth in contemporary culture; library kinds and their features, user groups and data requirement, etc. You would have found that there is an inherent continuity of intent in all these industries, i.e. providing an excellent library and data system. This basic approach has united all people operating in libraries and information / documentation centers to create partnerships to concentrate on their popular goals.

Associations of libraries are also known as learned communities. They encourage library motion growth in a nation. They strive to provide library and data facilities more effectively. Library organizations are also striving to advance the career and the practitioners in this phase. Professional associations in the areas involved are produced, by and for the experts. For example, librarians, library employees, library science educators, library customers and library organizations.

All of these industries are qualified for Library Association affiliation. By their effective cooperation and involvement in their programs and operations, an organization is what its employees think of it. As a new entrant to the industry, knowing how to engage in specialist organizations' an operation to help their ultimate cause is worthwhile for you.

3.7.1. Library associations, systems and programmes

You as a part in this program now aspire to apply to become a professional in library and data maintenance. You should be aware of your professional duties and obligations, i.e. striving to improve library and information systems and services and advance library and information science. After all, its employees are building up the image for career. Qualitative execution of responsibilities and compliance to ethical principles and norms are crucial for creditworthiness and strong professional standing. You will research how professional associations strive to promote these principles in the following parts.

3.7.2. Need and Importance of Professional Associations

A capable individual or a single organization, unlikely to do much to address broader and far-reaching specialist problems. Interested organizations need to take collective action. Professional associations act as a joint effort forum in this.

Development of libraries depends on skilled planning, foresight, comprehension and engagement. These problems are superior handled by partnerships of libraries than by external organizations. The profession's solidarity is therefore a requirement for collaborating and achieving outcomes for a popular cause. In reality, this solidarity is reflected in the power and efficiency of professional associations. Library organizations can assist spread the public library movement in a nation and provide stronger library operation if they perform their role well. They, indeed; help clarify library and data facilities ideas; and also make suitable suggestions to the correct corners.

3.7.4. Aims and objectives of library associations

Library associations are established with the following aims and objectives:

- To proclaim the library movement to disseminate knowledge and information in a country and

- To Contributing eventually to the growth of human resources;

- Working to enact public library laws, writing bills along progressive lines and centered on basic values; raising awareness of people's libraries to request the freedom of entry to public library facilities; mobilizing social pressure for safe library facilities growth;

- To Strive for the development of an embedded national library and information system centered on domestic strategy; draw the regulators ' focus to insufficiencies, imperfections, etc. in the current library infrastructure;

- To provide a common forum for library practitioners to share data, thoughts, feelings and knowledge, to improve wages, grades, terms of service, position of library practitioners, etc.;

- To maintain a strong social image of the library industry; to foster collaboration between libraries and library practitioners;;

- Resource sharing and avoiding replication of effort;

- Contributing to the development of manpower of library and information work, including tutoring and training, study, incentives, grants and rewards, etc.

3.7.5. Programmes and Activities of Library Associations

Library organizations typically conduct all or some of the programs and operations listed below, depending on their developmental stage. These organizations communicate from moment to moment with designed authorities, taking advantage of every conceivable chance for major growth in the nation of a library scheme. These duties are accomplished through advice, representation and assistance in legislative formation, strategy statement formation, recommendations, etc.

(i) Conferences : Organizing meetings, seminars, presentations, etc. to provide possibilities to encounter communicate and data swap, thoughts, feelings, and knowledge with library experts.

(ii) Library publicity : Organizing library week, exhibitions, and book fairs; contests, etc. to promote people's library awareness and practices of reading and teaching.

(iii) Service conditions : Using appropriate means to address management at all levels, issues related to improving salary grades, service conditions and the status of library professionals, the Library Association also helps to recruit library staff: they formulate ethics codes for library professionals in order to preserve high values of conduct and service.

(iv) Education : In order to complement university education in library and information science and ongoing schooling programs for operating practitioners, it is essential to conduct coaching classes. Operative is an authorizing agency in Library and Information Science Education to retain appropriate norms. Instituting prizes and bonuses is recognizing excellent library experts and library services efficiency.

(v) Publications : Library organizations release specialist literature such as a regular newspaper and newsletter, as well as voluntary papers such as procedures, directories, catalogues, bibliographies, lesson manuals, books, guides, etc.

(vi) Standards, services, research : Formulating norms, rules, and manuals on practices, processes, methods, instruments and facilities as a move towards encouraging library collaboration. Bibliographic projects are undertaken on their own and through external contracts. Offering consolatory and advisory services.

To conduct study studies of library equipment and services, user requirements, teaching and reading practices, book manufacturing, etc. to define strengths and faults in attempt to make needed measures to enhance the scheme.

(vii) Cooperation : Establishing collaboration with other nations with comparable objectives with international and domestic organizations. Maintaining book contact and publication business to address shared issues in library acquisitions.

3.7.6. A General Account of Library Associations in India

In India, we have historical records of earlier library organizations like the Baroda Library Association (1910), the Andhra Desa Library Association (1914), the Bengal Library Association (1927) and the Madras Library Association (1927). The Association of the Indian Library was established in 1933. There has been an rise in the amount of library organizations in the post-independence era.

We currently have a lot of library organizations at the domestic and state level. Special classifications of libraries, topics, areas and other special interests are also dedicated to organizations. The Govt, for instance. Indian Library Association (GILA), Indian Association of Library and Information Science Teachers (IATLIS), Indian Micrographic Congress (MIC); Information Science Society.

In adding to professional development, only a few organizations are involved. To become employees of library organizations, professionals are usually neutral. The reality that many countries which have not implemented library legislation points to the ineffectiveness of our library organizations. There is, however; range and need for our library organizations to function faster and perform faster. The previous parts describe two partnerships at all levels in India. The Indian Library Association and the Special Library and Information Center of Indian Association.

3.7.7. Indian Library Association (ILA)

The Association of the Indian Library was established in Calcutta in 1933. It is a licensed company that now has its office in Delhi. It is the country's leading national association that represents the entire library profession.

The Association's origin can be attributed back to the September 1933 All India Library Conference in Calcutta. All of the leading librarians of that period were instrumental in organizing the conference, whose main objective was to form the Association of the Indian Library. Seven All-India Library Conferences took place in distinct areas of the nation between 1933 and 1947. ILA publications included as an authorized organ two versions of the Indian Libraries Directory and a weekly newspaper called Library Bulletin. The Association experienced hectic and slow stages of operation after Independence.

There were 22 more All-India Library Conferences conducted until 1983, when ILA finished fifty years. The period's development was constant but not dramatic. It can be said that some of the ILA's projects have had an effect on the country's library growth. In 1992, for example, the ILA effectively arranged a Delhi meeting of the Indian Federation of Library Associations (IFLA). However, the library profession's aspirations have been far more than what has been accomplished throughout. The library industry is currently interested in making ILA powerful and efficient and there are indications of some advancement.

Objectives : The Association seeks to set high standards in the nation for librarianship and library facilities. And their objectives are:

(a) Promoting proliferation of libraries in the nation and enacting library laws.

(b) Improving library services.

(c) Development of book scientific schooling and book certification to maintain adequate educational norms.

(d) Improvement of wage, terms of delivery and position of library staff.

(e) Promotion of library and library professional collaboration.

(f) Promoting research and studying bibliography.

(g) State membership and other organizations of libraries.

(h) Cooperation with like-minded global and other domestic organizations.

(i) Publication of serial publications and other data dissemination journals.

(j) To create a common forum through the organization of conferences, seminars and meetings.

(k) Promotion and implementation of library and information systems management standards, standards, instructions, etc. and their facilities.

3.7.8. Organization

The Association's affiliation includes employers, lives and normal employees, as well as employees of institutions and associates. T 1e national assembly chooses a president, six vice presidents, a general secretary and council representatives up to 20 per 100 private representatives at the pace of one delegate and one delegate per 40 organizational representatives for a two-year period. There are 11 Sectional Committees, one delegate from each Member State Library Association, and the Association's ex-Presidents are also Council members. An Executive Committee composed of the Chair, one Vice-Chairman, the Secretary-General, the Treasurer, two Secretaries, P.R.O. and three representatives of the

Council. While the general body meets once a year, usually at the All India Library Conference, the council meets at least once a quarter and the executive committee meets as frequently as necessary. The Association's Annual Report and Accounts will be adopted at the General Body Meeting.

3.7.9. Activities

3.7.9.1. Conferences and Library Meetings

An-All India Library Conference takes position at some location in the nation every year. The guest organization is a college, organization, or partnership of local libraries. A National Seminar is component of the All-India Library Conference's program on one or more important and relevant topics. Moreover, from moment to moment national seminars on topical themes are also conducted.

The Association, mainly in Delhi, arranges presentations, round table conversations, etc. There is a regular one-month study circle gathering in Delhi to discuss technical topics. It is associated with libraries, other library organizations, etc. in programs that are usually arranged in November each year during the National Library Week.

3.7.9.2. Publications

The Association publishes a weekly newspaper named ILA Bulletin as an authorized organ and a car for publication knowledgeable papers submitted by library and information science experts. There is a system to award awards like the PV Verghese Prize, contributing to the ILA Bulletin for the finest post. To disseminate data of present concern to employees, the Association released ILA Newsletter each month. The Association has published the All India Library, a conference that contains the seminar papers debated at the conference, on a regular basis since 1978.

A pre-seminar amount holding the documents is also published in the event of ad hoc seminars. In 1985, it released the Indian Library Directory's fourth edition. A Directory of ILA Members was released in 1987. The Association regularly publishes its Annual Report and Account Statement. It is currently growing its publishing program. A NALANDA database of more than 10,000 libraries was established in 1995 (5336 Academic, 1470 Public and 3280 Special).

3.7.9.3. Continuing Education

Recently, the Association has launched a Continuing Education program for the advantage of workers. It has conducted a sequence of sessions on Computer Application to Library and Information Activities in various towns over the past century. For the future, more such programs are planned.

3.7.9.4. Consultancy

The Association has effectively hooked up and finished a technical handling scheme of approximately 35,000 specimens of a unique compilation for the National Administrative Academy of Lal Bahadur Shastri (LBS), Mussoorie. It gave up a comparable initiative for the Indira Gandhi National Center for the Arts beginning in November 1987.

3.7.9.5. Professional Issues

The Association addresses the problem of enacting library legislation to create the public library system with the State Governments at every conceivable chance. Repeated memoranda have been sent to persuade state governments to take intervention on library legislation. It has been involved in discussing issues with regulators, the University Grants Commission (UGC) and other management related to improving wage grades, terms of work, and the position of library practitioners. It took initiatives in the development of a national library service policy and held a seminar on the topic, as a result of which the Government of India appointed a Committee to prepare a National Library and Information System Policy. Certain amount of bills is generally enacted during the All India Library Conference on issues of specialist interest and concern, which the Association uses to implement with suitable officials.

3.7.9.6. Participation in Official Bodies

The ILA was depicted in the Seventh Plan Library and Informatics Modernization Working Group, which presented its study in July 1984. A draft was presented by the National Policy Committee on Library and Information System in May 1986; and the Review Committee to consider public librarians ' wage scales was established by the Government of India as recommended by the Fourth Pay Commission. It was called upon to present its view to the Mehrotra Committee, which under the Fourth Pay Commission regarded the wage scales for university library employees and librarians. The ILA is also depicted on the Good Offices Foundation of the Raja Ram Mohan Roy Library. Documentation Standards Committee, National Standards Bureau, Executive Committee-2 (NBS) Section Committee, National Commission and National Book Trust (NBT), World Book Fair Committee, etc.

3.7.9.7. Relations with Other Professional Bodies

ILA performs a major position in developing a consistent approach and a popular strategy on specialist problems of interest to all library organizations in the Joint Council of Library Associations (JOCLAI) in India. It has excellent operating relationships with IASLIC and partnerships of state libraries.

3.7.9.8. *Indian Association of Special and Information Centres (IASLIC)*

The Special Libraries and Information Centers Indian Association (IASLIC) was established in 1955. It was created in order to have an organization comparable to the Information Management Association in the United Kingdom and the Special Libraries Association in the United States in India.

IASLIC has risen in size and activity spectrum and has contributed in many respects to the enhancement of the country's special libraries and data centers. It has been recognized all these years for its periodic and thorough job.

Objectives : Following are major objectives of IASLIC:

(a) Encouraging and encouraging deliberate knowledge development, organisation and dissemination;

(b) Improving the performance and dissemination of library and data facilities;

(c) Coordination of operations and encouragement of shared collaboration and aid between special libraries; data facilities, etc.

(d) To act as an effective communication area for schools, data offices, paperwork facilities, etc., and

(e) To enhance the technical effectiveness of employees in unique schools, data facilities, etc.

(f) To Special library and documentation methods study center.

(g) To serve as a center for science, technical and other areas of data.

(h) To adopt such measures as may be incidental and conducive to the achievement of the Association's tasks.

3.7.10. Organization

IASLIC affiliation is made up of official employees, contributors, family and normal employees and employees of the institution. For a two-year period, the General Body chooses a President, six Vice-Presidents, a Secretary General, a Treasurer, two Joint Secretaries, two Assistant Secretaries, one Librarian, and 25 Council members. The Council shall appoint the Executive and Finance Committees from among its employees. The Association's job i ; allocated among six branches allocated to them with particular duties.

3.7.10.1. Meetings

IASLIC conducts a biennial seminar and convention in consecutive years at the location of guest organizations that are generally university libraries / library and information science agencies, institutions, organizations, etc. Special interest groups have lately been created in fields such as Industrial Information, Social Science Information, Computer Application and Humanities.

They gather to address issues of common interest at the moment of the quarterly meeting seminar. IASLIC organizes seminars, conferences, events, etc. from moment to moment. In Calcutta and other towns, it-has studied groups. The study circle sessions are conducted every month, discussing technical problems.

3.7.10.2. Publications

It is the formal organ, and in library and information science it performs taught papers. These are the (monthly) IASLIC Newsletter that disseminates data on the Association's operations as well as other documents of specialist concern; and the (annual) Indian Library Science Abstracts. In 1985, it released the second version of India's Directory of Special and Research Libraries. It has published a few monographs and a guide, code and glossary each. The Association frequently publishes its

Annual Report and Account and Membership List Statement. IASLIC annually honors the finest librari un of the year and the finest article in the IASLIC Bulletin.

3.7.10.3. *Education and Training*

IASLIC used to perform periodic teaching classes at the graduate stage in international subjects and library science in the beginning. Now it is involved on subjects such as Computer Applications, Indexing, and CDS / ISIS in a con6nuing education program. It performs short-term coaching courses in Calcutta and elsewhere for the advantage of operating experts. 3-4 workshops are organized each year.

3.7.10.4. *Bibliography and Translation Services*

IASLIC provides on-profit translating and database facilities to people and organizations. It holds a library dedicated to the literature of libraries and information sciences.

3.7.10.5. *Professional Issues*

The Association seeks to enhance customer requirements in unique libraries and data centers. It has created efforts to develop a code of ethics for librarianship in this regard. It brings issues that call for improvement and corrective action to the attention of authorities. It is concerned with noise library and information system scheduling and growth and encourages appropriate interventions in this respect. It took steps such as drafting an inter-library loan code for cooperation with libraries. It was quite responsive to the need for library experts to secure stronger wage scales, business circumstances and position. It brings library and information professionals together at all levels and speaks on professional issues as a whole for them.

3.7.10.6. *Relations with other Bodies*

IASLIC has a healthy relationship with the

Association of the Indian Library and other associations of libraries. In forming the Joint Council for Library Associations in India, it has taken a leading part. (JOCLAI). The implementation of the joint programs of this Joint Council for Library Associations in India requires an engaged stake. IASLIC is cooperating with the National Information System for Science and Technology (NISSAT) by taking up specific assignments and projects. It is represented in Indian Standards Institution, Documentation and Information Committee (ISIIEC2) (currently it is generally known as Bureau of Indian Standards).

3.7.10.7. Perspective for Future

IASLIC had satisfactory achievements in playing a leader / coordinator role in the department of the bibliography and information field.' It was now poised in the period ahead for assured growth and development to serve the cause of Indian special librarianship.

3.7.11. International Activities

Besides the biggest, the American Library Association (ALA) and its many branches, there are many professional associations for librarians. Specialized groups may be based on topic area, layout or both.

AALL: American Association of Law Libraries : "The American Association of Law Libraries was founded in 1906 to promote and enhance the legal and public community value of law libraries, to foster the profession of librarianship law, and to deliver leadership in the area of legal information."

AASL: American Association of School Librarians : The American Association of School Librarians (AASL), an American Library Association affiliate, "is the only domestic specialist affiliation organization centered on the requirements of college librarians and the college library society. We support the requirements of more than 7,000 college librarians in the U.S., Canada, and around the globe."

ACRL : Association of College & Research Libraries : A part of the American Library Association is the Association of College and Research Libraries (ACRL). ACRL is a professional association of academic librarians and other interested persons. It is dedicated to enhancing the capacity of academic libraries and information professionals to serve the higher education community's information needs and to improve learning, teaching and research. ACRL is the largest division of the American Library Association (ALA).

ALA: American Library Association : The American Library Association (ALA) is the world's earliest and biggest library association, supplying participants, librarians and book customers with data, media, activities and support tools. Founded on 6 October 1876 during the Centennial Exhibition in Philadelphia, ALA's task is to provide guidance in the growth, advancement and enhancement of libraries and librarianship.

ALCTS : Association for Library Collections & Technical Service : The American Library Association is a subsidiary of the Library Collections & Technical Service. "ALCTS enjoys a wealthy, 55-year record of assistance to its employees and aims to enhance the products and facilities it provides to its employees. With economic and tactical objectives strongly in position, ALCTS has a strong basis from which to grow its impact. ALCTS is the leading platform for information technology, comprising nearly 4,000 participants from across the United States and 42 nations worldwide.

ALSC: Association for Library Service to Children : Children's Library Service Association is an American Library Association affiliate. "The Association for Library Service to Children (ALSC) is the largest organization in the world dedicated to supporting and enhancing children's library service. From best practices and creative programming to continuing education and professional connections, ALSC members are innovators in the field of children's library service.

American Indian Library Association : "AILA was established in 1979 in combination with the White House Pre-Conference on Indian Library and Information Services on or close Reservations. At the moment, there was a growing consciousness that library facilities were insufficient for Native Americans. Individuals and government organizations started to fix the scenario. The American Indian Library Association, an associate of the American Library Association (ALA), is a member advocacy community that covers American Indians and Alaska Natives' library-related demands. Members are people and organizations involved in developing programs to enhance Indian library, social and information facilities in reserve libraries of college, publics and studies. AILA is also committed to disseminating information to the library community on the needs of Indian cultures, languages, values and information.

APALA : Asian Pacific American Librarians Association : Founded in 1980, the Asian Pacific American Librarians Association (APALA) was established in Illinois in 1981 and officially associated with the American Library Association (ALA) in 1982. A forerunner of APALA, the Asian American Librarians Caucus (AALC), was set up in 1975 as a debate unit of the ALA Library Outreach Services Bureau, showing the stake in mining library operations. APALA and AALC were structured and established before it by librarians of varied Asian and Pacific ancestry dedicated to operating together towards a prevalent objective: to establish an organization that would tackle the requirements of Asian Pacific American librarians and those serving Asian Pacific American groups.

Black Caucus of the American Library Association : "The American Library Association's Black

Caucus advocates the creation, advancement and enhancement of library facilities and assets for the African American society of the nation; and offers guidance for the training and professional development of African American librarians."

CALA: Chinese American Librarians Association : "The Chinese American Librarians Association (CALA) began in 1973 as the Mid-West Chinese American Librarians Association, a regional organization in Illinois. In 1974, the Chinese Librarians Association was established in California. In 1976, the Mid-West Chinese American Librarians Association was extended to become a domestic organization as the Chinese American Librarians Association. By 1979, in Northeast, Mid-West, Atlantic, Southwest and California, CALA had five branches. The Association of Chinese American Librarians and the Association of Chinese Librarians united in 1983. The fused organization maintains the English title of CALA and the Chinese name of the Chinese Librarians Association.

CARL: California Academic & Research Libraries : The purpose of CARL, as stated in its Constitution, is' to provide opportunities for the professional growth of its members by conducting workshops and organizing programs; to encourage the conversation of ideas and information on library cooperation and development; to disseminate educational information aimed at those working in academic and research libraries; and to support and, where appropriate, to facilitate the exchange of information on library cooperation and development;

CLA: California Library Association : "CLA is the Community for California Libraries CLA provides leadership in the development, promotion and enhancement of library, library, and library community services. In a fast-changing job market, we help members excel. We are a resource for learning new ideas and technology and we are active in influencing legislation that affects libraries and librarians.

CSLA California School Library Association : "CSLA promotes success in college library programs, creates professionals in the sector of school libraries and works with other academic officials to guarantee that all learners in California are efficient, accountable to consumers and producers of ideas and data."

LITA: Library and Information Technology Association : "The Library and Information Technology Association is the major organization comprising fresh experts, system librarians, library administrators, library schools, suppliers and anyone else interested in modern technology for library and data providing apps.

LLAMA: Library Leadership & Management Association : "The LLAMA Library Leadership and Management Association (Library Leadership and Management Association), a part of the American Library Association, can assist you gain the abilities and expertise to be a champion in your job. LLAMA equips library experts with a multitude of vibrant instruments to build powerful libraries and productive lives in line with ever-changing technological, political, financial and social circumstances. Our resources are tailored in all kinds of libraries to professionals of various cultural backgrounds and to all levels of library staff.

MLA: Medical Library Association : The Medical Library Association is a strong group where medical librarians can communicate with other peers and discover about "the recent instruments and education in health information management, study, and exercise" and become a champion in the medical librarian industry.

MLGSCA: Medical Library Group of Southern California & Arizona : MLGSCA is a branch of the Southern California (east of Fresno) and Arizona Medical Library Association. Join approximately 300 health science librarians and information professionals in networking, promote ongoing education, assist in the "development of library resources" and "facilitate cooperation between health science libraries."

PLA: Public Library Association : "With more than 9,000 employees, the Public Library Association (PLA) is one of the highest growing branches of the American Library Association (ALA), the world's first and biggest library association. Founded in 1944, PLA is a member-driven organization that continues to provide its employees and others concerned in advancing public library service with a varied program of communication, publishing, promotion, continuing education and programming.

REFORMA : The National Association to Promote Library & Information Services to Latinos and the Spanish Speaking : Found in 1971 as an associate of the American Library Association (ALA), REFORMA continually attempted to encourage the creation of library libraries to include Spanish-speaking and Latino-oriented products; to recruit and assist employees from more bilingual and bicult ıral library practitioners; to develop library facilities and programs that satisfy the requirements of the Latino society; Establishing a national information network and supporting individuals sharing our objectives; U.S. education. Latino people in terms of the accessibility and types of library services; and pushing their efforts to preserve existing library resource centers that serve Latinos' interests.

RUSA: Reference and User Services Association : "The Reference and User Services Association is accountable for encouraging and promoting success in the provision of overall library facilities and equipment, as well as the availability of reference and data facilities, collection development, users ' advice and resource exchange for every people in all types of libraries."

SLA: Special Libraries Association : "The Special Libraries Association (SLA) is a global non-profit organization for innovative IT professionals and their strategic partners. SLA serves more than 9,000 IT professionals in 75 countries, including corporate, academic and government information specialists. SLA promotes and strengthens its members through learning, encouragement and initiate networking."

United for Libraries : Friends of Libraries U.S.A. (FOLUSA) and the Association of Library Trustees and Advocates (ALTA) joined forces on 1 February 2009 to become an expanded ALA division known as the Association of Library Trustees, Advocates, Friends and Foundations, now United for Libraries. Through this partnership, United for Libraries brings together the voices of libraries to speak on behalf of the library information access. United for Libraries is a domestic network of passionate library followers who think in schools ' significance as societies and universities ' cultural and academic centers. For libraries, no one has a greater voice than those who use them, lift and regulate cash for them. By uniting these voices, library supporters will become a real force at the local, state, and national levels.

YALSA: Young Adult Library Services Association : A section of the American Library Association is the Young Adult Library Services Association (YALSA). YALSA is a "domestic organization of librarians, library employees and proponents whose task is to grow and reinforce library facilities for adolescents aged 12-18. YALSA develops the ability of libraries and librarians to participate, represent and empower adolescents through its member-driven promotion, exploration and professional development projects."

3.8. INFORMATION AND DOCUMENTATION ORGANIZATIONS : ROLE OF UNESCO, DESIDOC, NASSDOC, RRRLF, UGC

In India and overseas, many organizations, organizations and organizations are working to promote, coordinate and develop library and data facilities. Some of these are financed by the state and others are skilled organizations and charitable organizations. These act as professionals, advisory bodies, funding agencies and providers of services, etc. It is hard to cover all such types of national and international organizations; therefore, some of the well-established organizations are described in this Unit. These include the United Nations Educational, Scientific and Cultural Organization (UNESCO), the University Grants Commission (UGC), the Raja Ram Mohun Roy Library Foundation (RRRLF), the National Documentation Center for Social Sciences (NASSDOC), the Defense Scientific Information and Documentation Center (DESIDOC), library and data networks, for example. The development of library and information services, INFLIBNET, DELNET, CALIBNET, INFONET, etc.

3.8.1. International Organisations

3.8.1.1. *United Nations Educational, Scientific and Cultural Organization (UNESCO)*

The United Nations Educational, Scientific and Cultural Organization (UNESCO) law, adopted on November 16, 1945, went into effect on November 4, 1946, after 20 nations including India had ratified it. Today, UNESCO acts as an ideology laboratory and a standard setter to forge global contracts on evolving ethical problems. It also serves as a clearing house–for information and knowledge dissemination and sharing–while helping Member States build their human and institutional capacity in a variety of fields. UNESCO promotes international cooperation in the fields of education, science, culture and communication between its 193 Member States and 6 Associate Members. Article I Clause 1 Sub-clause (c) of its Constitution provides that' the Organization shall retain, boost and disseminate understanding by ensuring the preservation and preservation of the world's heritage of novels, pieces of art and historical and scientific landmarks and by recommending the required cooperation to the nations involved;

Freedom, wealth, and social and individual growth are basic natural ideals. Only by the ability of well-informed citizens to exercise their democratic rights and play an active role in society will they be achieved. Constructive involvement and democratic development rely on adequate education as well as open and universal access to knowledge, thinking, language and data. The public library, the local information portal, offers a fundamental situation for person and social communities 'continuous teaching, autonomous decision-making and cultural growth. Adopted in 1994, the Public Library Manifesto proclaims the belief of UNESCO in the public library as a living force for education, culture and information and as an essential agent for the promotion of peace and spiritual welfare through the minds of men and women. Accordingly, UNESCO promotes domestic and local authorities to promote and openly participate in public library growth. To be the core of public library services should be the following key missions related to information, literacy, education and culture::

- Create and reinforce learning practices in young age of childhood;
- Supporting person and self-conducted education at all stages as well as normal education;
- Providing possibilities for artistic personal development;
- Stimulating children and young people's imagination and creativity;
- Promoting cultural heritage consciousness, art appreciation, science accomplishments and innovation;
- Providing access to all performing arts' cultural expressions;

- Favoring intercultural dialog and promoting cultural diversity;

- Fostering the oral tradition;

- Ensure access to all kinds of community information for citizens;

- Providing local businesses, organizations and interested groups with appropriate data facilities;

- Facilitate the growth of computer knowledge and data abilities;

- Support and involvement in literacy activities and programs for all age groups and, where necessary, initiate such activities.

The School Library Manifesto passed by UNESCO in 1999 seeks to identify and promote the position of college collections and information centers in allowing learners to obtain teaching instruments and material that enable them to create their complete capacity; to proceed studying throughout their life; and to create educated choices. For the growth of literacy, information literacy, teaching, learning and society, the aforementioned are crucial:

- Support and enhance instructional objectives as described in the task and schedule of the school;

- Develop and sustain the habit and pleasure of reading and learning in children and the use of libraries throughout their lives;

- Offering possibilities for interactions in knowledge, comprehension, fantasy and creation and use of data;

- Supporting all learners in teaching and practicing data assessment and use abilities, irrespective of type, format or medium, including sensitivity to communications within the society;

- Providing access to local, regional, national and global resources and opportunities for learners to have different ideas, opinions and experiences;

- Organizing cultural and social awareness and sensitivity activities;
- Working with students, teachers, administrators and parents to fulfill the school's mission; proclaiming the concept that intellectual freedom and access to information are essential for effective and accountable citizenship and democratic participation;
- Promoting learning and the college library's resource and facilities to the entire college group and beyond.

Activities

Access to Information : UNESCO aims to improve access to information and knowledge for individuals and organizations. It seeks to create conditions conducive to free information flow. High on its agenda is universal access to information. It creates awareness and develops management tools to strengthen libraries in order to achieve universal access to information.

Archives : Archives are important components that help improve access to information for both the general public and specialized groups. UNESCO has contributed to strengthening these types of services since its inception. The development of information technology and, in particular, the Internet, networking, cooperation and digitization substantially alter the functions of information and knowledge acquisition, storage and dissemination. UNESCO pays particular attention to underdeveloped countries so that they do not lag behind advances in technology. In the archive field, UNESCO, through its Management Program for Records and Archives-RAMP (established in 1979) aims at:

- To raise awareness of the importance of records and archives for the safeguarding and development of national heritage;

- Supporting Members of States in setting up efficient records and archives management infrastructures through standardization, archival legislation, training and infrastructure improvement (buildings and equipment);

- Promoting international discussions on major archival issues.

Memory of the World : In 1992, UNESCO set up the World Program Memory. It gives access to the world's documentary heritage. The program was intended to protect and preserve documents endangered as a result of natural or manmade disasters.

In 1993, an International Advisory Committee (IAC) was formed to develop an action plan that would give UNESCO the role of coordinator and catalyst to sensitize governments, international organizations and foundations, and to foster partnerships for project implementation. The general program guidelines were drawn up by contract with IFLA (International Library Associations Federation) and ICA (International Archives Council). Through its National Commissions, UNESCO prepared a list of endangered library and archive holdings and a world list of national cinema heritage. A series of pilot projects were started under the program using contemporary technology to reproduce original documentary heritage on other media. (These included, for example, a 13th-century Radzivill Chronicle CD-ROM tracing the origins of Europe's peoples, and Memoria de Iberoamerica, a joint microfilming newspaper project involving seven Latin American countries). These projects enhanced access to and contributed to the preservation of this documentary heritage. It also includes the Vedas which is one of the world's first literatures to be produced.

Community Multimedia Centres : The UNESCO International Multimedia Center Initiative (CMCs) promotes community empowerment and addresses the digital divide by combining community-based broadcasting with the Internet and related technologies. A CMC combines local community radio with community telecenter facilities (internet and e-mail computers, telephone, fax and photocopying services) in local languages. The low-cost and easy-to-operate radio not only informs, educates and entertains, but also empowers the community by giving the voiceless a strong public voice, thereby promoting greater accountability in public affairs.

Radio-browsing programs: Broadcasters search the network in response to questions from listeners and discuss with studio guests on air the contents of pre-selected websites.

Multimedia development databases: The CMC can progressively construct its own database of materials that meet the information needs of the community.

Open learning: The CMC exists in areas such as education and training, health and income generation to meet development needs.

E-Governance : E-governance is the use of ICT by various social personalities with the goal of improving their access to information and building their capacity. The main ongoing UNESCO e-governance activity is a cross-cutting E-Governance Capacity-Building project. The objective of this project is to promote the use of ICT tools in municipalities to improve good governance by developing training modules for local decision-makers in Africa and Latin America.

Information Processing Tools : UNESCO develops, maintains and distributes two interrelated database management software packages (CDS / ISIS) and data mining / statistical analysis packages (IDAMS) free of charge.

CDS / ISIS is a widespread system for storing and retrieving information. The variant of Windows may operate on a given desktop or network in a local region.

The client / server parts of Java ISIS enable distant Internet database management and are accessible for Windows, Linux and Macintosh. In addition, GENISIS enables users to create HTML Web forms for searching for CDS / ISIS databases. The ISIS-DLL offers an API to develop apps depending on CDS / ISIS.

IDAMS is a package of numerical data processing and analysis software. It offers a broad variety of equipment for information processing and validation and a broad variety of traditional and sophisticated statistical techniques. Interactive elements enable multidimensional charts to be constructed, information graphical discovery and evaluation of time series. WinIDAMS technology (IDAMS for Windows 32-bit operating system) is accessible in English, French, Portuguese and Spanish as well as paperwork. IDIS is a instrument for CDS / ISIS and IDAMS immediate information exchange.

Knowledge and training is as important as the ools themselves in the use of information processing tools. In the use of CDS / ISIS and IDAMS, UNESCO currently offers various forms of traditional training. A computerized tutorial "How to work with Win-IDAMS" is available in English, French, Portuguese and Spanish for both stand-alone PC configurations and virtual internet courses.

Public Domain Information : UNESCO heavily encourages entry to data on the public domain, also recognized as' data commons.' The use of data on the public domain does not infringe any legal right or infringe any other community privileges (such as indigenous rights) or confidentiality obligations. Information in the public domain refers to the realm of all works or objects of related rights that can be exploited by everyone without any authorization, for example because protection is not granted under national or international law or because the term of protection has expired or because there is no international instrument guaranteeing protection in the case of foreign works or objects UNESCO calls on Member

States to acknowledge and enact the requirement of full internet disclosure to government and government documents, including data appropriate to people in a contemporary democratic culture, with owing regard for confidentiality, privacy and national security issues, as well as intellectual property rights, to the point that they extend to the use of such data. International organizations should acknowledge and promulgate the obligation of each State to communicate vital cultural or economic data.

E-Heritage : Heritage is "our heritage from the past, what we are living with today, and what we are passing on to future generations". A heritage is something that is passed from generation to generation because it is valued. Examples of cultural heritage are: sites, objects, and intangible things that have cultural, historical, aesthetic, archaeological, scientific, ethnological, or anthropological value to individuals and groups. The concept of natural heritage is also very familiar: physical, biological and geological characteristics; habitats of plants or animal species and valuable areas on scientific or esthetic grounds or from a conservation point of view.

More and more of the cultural and educational resources of the world are being produced, distributed and digitally accessed. Born-digital heritage is now part of the cultural heritage of the world online, including electronic journals, World Wide Web pages or online databases. However, there is technical obsolescence and physical decline in digital information. Internet instability is an additional risk of accumulating knowledge in html format. The need to safeguard this relatively new form of documentary heritage calls for international consensus on its collection, preservation and dissemination resulting in the adoption of the "UNESCO Charter on the Preservation of the Digital Heritage" Guidelines accompanying the Charter to adapt and extend current policies, legal frameworks and archival procedures so that this new form of heritage The program of UNESCO aims to preserve and disseminate valuable archive holdings and collections of libraries around the world.

Digital Heritage consists of enduring value computer-based materials that should be maintained for generations to come. Digital heritage emanates from various communities, sectors, industries, and regions. Not all digital materials are of enduring value, but those that require active preservation approaches when it comes to maintaining the continuity of digital heritage.

According to the Digital Heritage Preservation Charter of UNESCO :

*   Human knowledge or expression resources, whether cultural, educational, scientific and administrative or technical, legal, medical and other information, are increasingly created digitally or converted from existing analog resources into digital form.

*   Digital materials include, among a wide and growing range of formats, texts, databases, still and moving images, audio, graphics, software and web pages. They are often ephemeral and require careful manufacturing, maintenance and management.

*   Many of these assets have enduring value and meaning and are therefore a legacy that should be protected and maintained for present and future generations. This heritage can be found in any language, any part of the world, and any area of knowledge of human or expression.

General Information Program : The General Information Program was created to bring together two series of activities that have been carried out separately by UNESCO so far: the UNISIST Intergovernmental Program on Scientific and Technical Information, on the one hand, and NATIS, on the other hand, the concept of integrated national information related to documentation, libraries and archives. The practice of the General Information Program is driven by the General Information

Programme's Intergovernmental Council, whose representatives are chosen by the General Conference of UNESCO. In the interest of education, science, culture and communication, the Intergovernmental Council for PGI is the authority responsible for ensuring the continuity of past UNESCO activities in the field of information and the future development of the General Information Program.

In particular, the Council, made up of 36 Member States elected at its regular sessions by the General Conference, is responsible for:

- Guiding the design and layout of the UNESCO General Information Program, in specific by making suggestions to the General Conference on the Medium-Term Plan and its overhaul and the design of potential programs and plans;

- Study of proposals for program developments and changes;

- Recommend guidelines for the different operations or organizations of operations that constitute the program;

- Review of the results achieved and identify the key areas of international cooperation;

- Encourage and assist Member States to participate and coordinate their activities in the UNESCO General Information Program;

- Reviewing other UNESCO data operations and recommending greater cooperation of those operations to the Director-General;

- Searching for voluntary contributions, financial or in kind, to supplement the resources available for the implementation of the General Information Program under the regular budget.

Since 2001, Information for All Program (IFAP) has replaced the General Information Program. IFAP seeks to overcome the society's digital divide. It advocates splitting information for all people on the wrong side. The program is concerned with the needs of women, youth, the elderly and the non-capable persons.

The Information for All Programme seeks to:

- Promote international reflection and debate on information society's ethical, legal and societal challenges;
- Promote and extend public access to information by organizing, digitizing and preserving information;
- Support for communication, information and informatics training, continuing education and learning;
- Promote local content production and foster indigenous knowledge availability through basic literacy and ICT literacy training;
- Promote the application of international standards and best practices in the fields of communication, information and computer science of UNESCO; and
- Promote local, national, regional and international networking of information and knowledge.

Information for Development : One of the challenges IFAP faces is to explain the value of information in addressing development issues to governments and communities. The UN Millennium Declaration's objectives link development and poverty eradication with good governance and transparency. Information Alphabetization is one of those competencies that empower people to access and use information. In all aspects of life, it enables lifelong learning and decision-making. In the digital world, information literacy requires individuals to have technology and media skills. IFAP promotes actions to raise awareness of the importance of information literacy and to support projects that build users' literacy skills. An integral component of information literacy is the ethical use of information. IFAP works with its partner institutions to promote ethical use of information.

Information Accessibility : "Accessibility to information includes the many issues surrounding the availability, accessibility and affordability of information, such as multilingualism, metadata, interoperability, open source software, open content, Creative Common licenses as well as addressing the special needs of disabled people."

Divide was created as a result of unequal information availability among the various cross-sections of society. Economic concerns also create barriers in society to free access to information. In this direction, UNESCO has encouraged global efforts. Projects in areas like Free and Open Source Software (FOSS), Open Educational Resources (OER), etc. have been granted results.

3.8.1.2. *University Grants Commission (UGC)*

The University Grants Commission (UGC) is a statutory organization set up by Parliament's Act of 1956. This is a national body designed to coordinate, determine and maintain university education standards. The UGC serves as a vital connection between the Union and state governments and higher learning institutions. Besides giving grants to universities and colleges, the UGC also advises union and state governments on the necessary measures to improve university education. It also frames regulations such as those on the minimum teaching standards and teacher qualifications on the advice of subject specialists and academics with whom it interacts frequently in connection with program formulation, evaluation and monitoring.

Section 12 of the UGC Act provides that, in consultation with the universities concerned, the Commission shall take whatever steps it considers fit for the promotion and coordination of university education and for the maintenance of teaching, examination and research standards. The Commission implements schemes / programs to promote excellence and to improve the standards of higher learning institutions.

The Commission has also played a major role in promoting library and information services in these universities and colleges as an apex body in maintaining higher education in the country. It also set up and set up a number of libraries / information centers / study centers and committees to provide quality library and information activities education and service. Some of these are:

Financial Assistance to University and College Libraries : Universities and colleges, including Central Universities, State Universities, Deemed Universities, Government and affiliated colleges, receive grants to build libraries to meet the demands of students, teachers and research scholars. The Commission provides substantial subsidies to purchase books and newspapers.

Other infrastructure facilities such as library buildings also receive grants for furniture and equipment in each five-year plan period. It also introduced a' book bank scheme in colleges and universities by providing' grants to purchase multiple copies of expensive textbooks recommended across all disciplines. The aim of this scheme was to provide long-term textbooks by charging nominal deposits to poor, needy and deserving students for home study. UGC support no longer operates this scheme.

(i) Curriculum Development Committee (CDC) on Library and Information Science : In 1990, the UGC established the Library and Information Science CDC to restructure the study courses. The committee framed in its recommendations, guidelines for LIS schools, covering admission policy, students and strength of the faculty, teaching methodology, teaching assistances, IT application, etc. It also set up a committee called the UGC Panel in Library and Information Science to propose changes to be introduced in the training and education of LIS courses.

(ii) Establishment of National Information Centres : The aim of establishing National Information Centers in specialized areas is to provide improved access to information and to provide bibliographic support in their respective fields to teachers and research scholars. Three such centers were established and computer databases were developed to render reference and information services, documentation services, and current services of awareness.

(iii) Establishment of INFLIBNET : As a project of the Inter University Center for Astronomy and Astrophysics (IUCA) Pune in April 1991, the UGC set up an Information and Library Network (INFLIBNET) program with headquarters in Ahmedabad. The INFLIBNET Program aims to establish a national network of libraries and information centers in higher learning institutions including universities, colleges, research and development institutions and national organizations such as CSIR, ICMR, ICSSR, ICAR, DOE, etc.

INFLBNET is a network of libraries and bibliographic information centers for computer communication. It is a cooperative network program for pooling, sharing, and optimizing library and information center resources, facilities, and services, both in the university system and in the R&D complex. It provides students, academies and researchers with access to information through the rendering of various information and documentation services such as (a) database service (b) catalog-based service (c) document delivery service (d) communication-based service and (e) collection development.

(iv) Modernization of university libraries : Recent developments in information and communication technology and its usefulness have forced university libraries to computerize their services and connect to various network programs such as INFLIBNET in order to provide their users with a fast, efficient and reliable computerized information service. During the financial years 1994-95 and 1995-96, the UGC provided special financial assistance to central university libraries (2 crore rupees) and university libraries established prior to independence (50 lakh rupees). The main goal was to computerize and connect library activities to the INFLIBNET program. The use of the fund provided for the purpose is to cover the following costs:

- Computer system purchase, monitor, printer, terminals, software, etc.
- Computer, furniture, electrical and air conditioning equipment.
- Mode, telephone and nearest mode connection.
- Information scientist's appointment.
- Data entry support work.
- Purchase and processing of books, newspapers, A / V.
- Conservation of data entry (modernization).
- Training of staff.

(v) National Review Committee on University and College Libraries : The purpose of setting up such a committee is to review the use of grants from Rs. 2 crores and Rs.50 lakhs respectively to central universities and some state university libraries. Secondly, to organize a status report of university and college libraries in India and finally to create a strategy plan / guideline for the future for these university and college libraries to function smoothly.

3.8.1.3. *Raja Rammohun Roy Library Foundation (RRRLF)*

The Raja Rammohun Roy Library Foundation (RRRLF) was founded in May 1972 by the Department of Culture, Government of India to distribute library services throughout the country in cooperation with state governments, territorial union administrations and field-based organizations. It is a central autonomous organization set up and funded by the Government of India's Ministry of Culture. It is the Government of India's nodal agency to support public library services and systems and promote the country's public library movement. RRRLF's supreme body of policy making is called the Foundation. It consists of members from eminent educators, librarians, administrators, and senior officials nominated by the Government of India. There are 22 members of the Foundation. The Chairman of RRRLF is the Minister of the Culture Department, Government of India or his nominee. Through a machine called the State Library Planning Committee (SLPC / SLC), established in each state at the instance of the foundation, the foundation works in close association and active cooperation with various state governments and union territorial administrations. A certain amount is required to be contributed by the foundation to participate in its programs; RRRLF headquarters are located in Kolkata, Mumbai, New Delhi and Chennai with four zonal offices.

Objectives : RRRLF acts as a public library growth agency, an educational and consultant organization and a funding body in India. Some of its important goals are:

- To Promote the country's library action motion;
- To help build a national library system and specify national library policies;
- Providing libraries with economic and technical help;
- Provide monetary help for library development organizations, regional or domestic;
- To Publish and behave as a place of ideas and data on library development in India and overseas;
- Promoting studies on library development issues; and
- Advise the state on all issues concerning the growth of libraries in the nation.

3.8.1.4. *National Social Science Documentation Centre (NASSDOC)*

As a unit of the Indian Council for Social Science Research (ICSSR), N.\SSDOC was created in 1969. Its goal is to provide library and data help facilities to social science scientists operating in educational institutions, independent study organizations, public agencies, business and industry decision making, scheduling and study divisions, etc. Among its tasks are:

- Provide advice to research institutes backed by ICSSR regional branch and ICSSR support branch;
- Providing study grants for PhD learners to collect research content from separate archives in multiple areas of India;
- Financial support for bibliographic and paperwork initiatives;
- Providing paper distribution services through the provision of inter-library credits and publications or photocopying of papers; and
- Organizing short-term coaching classes for study researchers, cultural researchers, librarians and IT experts to get them to know the recent data and modern technologies.

It has a high range of number of contact, bibliographies, academic theses, ICSSR-funded study design records and publications and other records. The library maintains ICSSR sized and unrated journals including those for which publishing subsidies have been given by the Council. Documents are only accessible in the library facilities for advice. The warehouse for borrowing is only expanded to enrolled participants. It subscribes to some 450 present Indian / Foreign newspapers, including ICSSR newspapers and other cultural science abstracting and indexing publications. The library has over 11,000 bound volumes of newspapers, census records and other journals from the govt.

NASSDOC library provide the following services.

Facility for consultation: Research academics traveling NASSDOC can view multiple internet libraries, International Political Science Abstracts, Socio File, Psycinfo, etc.

Reference Service: Reference queries obtained by employees in individual, via e-mail, telephone, fax.

Referral Service: Research scientists are linked to other institutions / libraries in the event of non-availability of information in the classroom.

Literature Search: NASSDOC has a decent range of bibliographic data, including internet and CD-ROM databases, both in published and digital type. It has also developed its own written and digital records.

These libraries are used to find literature on different subjects. Document Delivery Service: NASSDOC offers its library and other libraries and organizations in India and overseas with records of study products.

Bibliographic Service: On request, bibliographic service is given. This system is given in two types, namely bibliographic quotes and the other bibliographic reference together with an abstract or summary of the document's reasoning material.

Union Catalog of Social Science Periodicals and Series in India: NASSDOC undertook the federation catalog job in 1970. The full database was released in 32 parts with information of keeping documents of 31,125 publications in 550 libraries, 17 countries, and two regions of the union. The National Library, Kolkata, has a distinct collection.

Union Catalog of CD-ROM Social Science Library collections in India: This catalog includes data about 132 CD-ROM databases accessible in 40 main universities and data centers in India. It offers information on the CD-ROM database name, frequency, short annotation, manufacturer / vendor, and holding data.

Directory of So ial Science Libraries and Information Centers in India: The Directory offers details of libraries and data centers connected to public depaitments, research and teaching institutions under multiple ministries, colleges and independent organs, companies, business and trade, etc. in the area of cultural scientific and related fields. References from their mother organizations are given to libraries with an autonomous title. Each registration offers book name, telephone number, personnel power, sample form, schedule, topic information, computerization information, equipment and services offered such as photocopying, bibliography, interlibrary lending, internet libraries, literature query, transcription, etc. The data in the folder makes it easier for Indian universities and information centers to cooperate and share resources. The diet includes 447 establishments.

Directory of Social Science Research and Training Institutions in India. The Directory offers a extensive roster of about 450 education and coaching organizations in India. It includes information on study fields, major accomplishments, unique equipment, present study initiatives, journals, sort of employees, compilation and services of libraries, relationships with domestic and international organizations, and full address with telephone, telex, fax and e-mail.

Directory of India's Asian Social Science Research and Training Institutes / Organizations: it is a register of India's Asian Studies education and education institutions. The amount of these is 42. Each registration offers data on the title, location of the organization, form of organization, sort of employees, goals and goals, operations, organization of parents, journals, location and amount of teaching classes, compilation of libraries and the institution's services and equipment.

3.8.1.5. Defence Scientific Information and Documentation Centre (DESIDOC)

DESIDOC became the Scientific Information Bureau (SIB) in 1958. It was subsequently a Defense Science Laboratory (DSL) branch where it became the Defense Science Center. With increased activities, SIB was reorganized in 1967 and named the Defense Scientific Information and Documentation Center (DESIDOC). On 29 July 1970, it became a self-accounting department and one of the Organization for Defense Research and Development (DRDO) labs. It offers the DRDO headquarters and its numerous laboratories throughout the nation with science and technical data depending on its library and other data assets. Today, DESIDOC functions as a key data repository for DRDO labs dedicated to the development of defense technologies spanning multiple fields such as aerospace, armaments, aerospace, fighter cars, technology systems, equipment, rockets, sophisticated computation and modeling, unique equipment, marine systems, health sciences, teaching, data systems and DESIDOC's primary goals are to:

- Function as a key tool for providing science and technical data, paperwork, classroom, reprography, conversion to DRDO HQrs, laboratories, institutions and the coordination of their science data programs;

- Develop the Defense Science and Technology Information System;

- Provide science data preparation and customer education programs;

- Offer services and referrals; and

- Publish DRDO science and technical papers, texts and monographs.

Defense Science Library (DSL) : DSL is a distinctive specialized library that addresses scientists' data requirements in defense science and technology. It has a wealthy range of micro and macro topics on defense science and technology. It offers a distinctive setting for both traditional and modern library configuration. It has comics, newspapers, attached files, technical records, microfilms, microfiches, graphs, atlases, tables, movies, audio tapes, audio clips, etc. Internet / Intranet, Online, CD-ROM / DVD devices occupy the center stage of a modern library in the ever-expanding situation of information and communication technology. DSL, with its electronic library initiatives, also achieving new targets.

CONCLUSION

Information is a essential asset for a country's socio-economic, cultural, scientific, and technological growth. Countries, making optimal use of this essential asset, are making progress towards rapid growth and a powerful domestic economy. Libraries, data centers organize data resource, collect and disseminate correct data and provide the customers within the infrastructure and equipment accessible. Developed countries have reinforced their data foundation by realizing the position of data in domestic growth for a long time. Many developing countries, such as India, are also creating attempts to build the country's noise data foundation. In this assignment contribute many organizations, organizations, professional bodies. International organizations have a wealth of experience in sharing their ideas and technical knowledge in information-related operations. This may, to some level, decrease the gulf between demand and data availability.

REVIEW QUESTIONS

1.   What do you think the needs for the importance of professional associations?

2.   How to improve the programs and activities of library associations.

3.   Any objective of library associations should be changed?

4

Library And Society

LEARNING OBJECTIVES

- This unit will introduce the notions of information and knowledge societies and examine in some detail their basic traits and characteristics.

- Outlining the principal differences between knowledge societies and pre-knowledge societies and explaining the major issues that need to be addressed in becoming a knowledge society.

4.1. KNOWLEDGE SOCIETY

Since time immemorial, knowledge has been central to growth and development. A main occupation of humanity has been the ability to invent and innovate and create new knowledge for the development of new products, processes and services that improve the quality of life. However, the words "Knowledge Society" and "Knowledge Economics" have been invented more lately. It is essential to distinguish between knowledge and data for a correct comprehension. Knowledge enables its owners to act intellectually or physically. Knowledge is a question of knowledge. Instead, information takes the form of structured and formatted data that remain passive and inert and used for interpretation and processing by those with the knowledge required.

Peter Drucker likely used the word "information society" in 1969 for the first time. It is not just a coincidence that the concept has emerged in conjunction with such ideas as the learning society, lifelong learning, etc. Every society was, in a wide sense, a knowledge society, as every society must have its wisdom. However, in the current context the word often references a culture in which knowledge, in contrast to societies in which capital and labor still dominate, is a main factor of financial productivity. The 'Knowledge society' as it was understood today and the previous knowledge societies are another important differentiation. The focus is now on human rights, inclusiveness, and involvement of all sectors of society. A knowledge society produces stocks and applies expertise for its people's prosperity and well-being.

As soon as 1914, 100 years ago, there was a very strongly associated term ' post-industrial society.' In his well-known book, "The Coming of the PostIndustrial Society" it was Daniel Bell who revived its use. It described the newly emerging social-economic phenomenon by emphasizing that new buildings of the ancient industrial era have been substituted by fresh ones instead of by concentrating on their "content." This word was the most frequently used prior to an all-acceptation of "data culture" The information society is a strongly associated word and is now commonly used. Although often interchangeably the terms "Information Society" and "Know-how Society," there is a distinction that requires to be understand.

The concept of "Information Society" as it is currently understood is mainly based on the technological breakthroughs resulting from the ICT revolution. While the Internet is the key concept of the knowledge society, as a government network and as platform for a fair and universal access to information resources, its social, political, cultural and even ethical consequences are much wider. Plans to bring about a culture of knowledge should be based on the understanding that control of knowledge and access to information can also go hand in hand with severe inequalities, exclusion and social conflict even in today's technologically-driven culture. Ideally a real community of understanding should include all its members and foster fresh forms of solidarity between current and future generations. Where information is a government good, accessible to each person, nobody must be excluded from knowledge societies.

"The Information Society is the building block for wise societies," says Abdul Waheed Khan from UNESCO's Communication and Information Division. While the idea of an "data society" has to do with the notion of "technological development," the notion of "knowledge communities" involves a more pluralistic and developmental aspect of social, cultural, economical, political and institutional development. I think that the idea of "knowledge society," because it better captures the complexity and dynamism of changing things that are taking place, is more preferable to that of "information society." This knowledge is important not only for economic development but for empowerment and the development of all social sectors.

The following can be found in the discussions above:

- The word information society may not necessarily mean the same idea for everyone. It is therefore appropriate to consider the pluralistic, heterogeneous and diverse nature of societies in the context of information societies. Another significant aspect is that a nation must consider and use technologies adapted to its growth priorities when moving towards an data culture;

- The term information society also refers to a society in which information / knowledge is a public good, not a commodity or a private property. Information communicating is a participatory and interactive process.

- Not in telecoms and in information science but instead in education, science, innovation, the (new) economy, content and culture, will the real dimensions of the informational society be apparent.

4.2. THE INFORMATION SOCIETY AND KNOWLEDGE SOCIETY

The word "Information Society" (or data age) has reflected the changes brought about at the end of the 20th century by technological development and globalization. The notion of the Information Society summarizes the new world order, which depends progressively on the situation of the countries, their strength, richness and impact. In the growth of ICTs, the quantity of data accessible and the velocity and ease at which it can be spread have increased enormously. Omekwu (2005) pointed out that data is becoming an information society as a result of its growing importance through technological growth and implementation. Information is more and more viewed as a commodity to be purchased, possessed, purchased and sold. This was pointed out by Issa (2003) as defining an Information Society as a trade commodity in which information is viewed. An item that is available for purchase and sale at a specified cost in the data industry. An essential commodity for domestic growth. Consequently, no equal access to data is available to everyone. Instead, globalization has acquired an increased gap betwee i the facts. A gap between the wealthy, the privileged and the unprivileged. Information can be regarded as something and thus a commodity, the dominant understanding and the term Information Society / Age can be seen. But data that develops in contact with the individuals looking for it can be seen in terms of impacts. This view takes the concept of knowledge and learning nearer to the concept.

In order to develop knowledge societies, the creation of an information culture has created some needed circumstances. But there are fundamental distinctions: the knowledge society is more empowering and inclusive than the data society. We talk of the information society, but knowledge societies as they are pluralistic as well. While the ICTs focus on netwerking and connectivity, the knowledge communities use it to open access for all to enhance the utilization of knowledge for all types of human development in all its types. Their purpose is not just to create a society that everyone wants, that is to build a knowledge society, but to use them to build a society that everyone wants and that is to know.

As an option to an "data culture" in some scholarly circles, the term "knowledge society" ("society of understanding") was first used by Peter Drucker in 1969.

Knowledge society involving all members of a community in creating and using knowledge is a more complete and richer idea with a focus on content, data development, distribution and use in culture. The collection, processing and allocation are not just the consequence.

Knowledge society needs to be applied, experienced, and judged. The idea was born in close association with the concept of culture and lifelong learning. While the UNESCO study of 2005 states that knowledge control is component of a mechanism promoting inequality, exclusion and social conflict, all societies are information societies in certain ways. The European Age of Enlightenment spreads requirements for democracy, openness, equality, liberty, understanding and education and other fields of life. This has resulted in the increased spread of knowledge through books and printing, and the development of schools and universities, and education to more citizens. Humanity has learned how to mass-produce information through latest technological innovations, but how is that information going to be used? Using ICTs provides us with fresh opportunity for the realization of the concept of democracy and liberty of speech to attain equal and universal access of information and real change in a government forum of information.

According to the study of UNESCO (2005), these fresh advances are to "be the backbone of real and viable knowledge societies." Societies which create institutions and organisations that enable individuals and data to be developed without limitations and open the way to mass production and mass use of all types of knowledge are knowledge societies.

The knowledge society has been described by Lor and Britz (2006) as a society which works within the information economic paradigm. The main intrinsic to manufacturing and innovation is human capital.

The five characteristics of knowledge society were listed in Dike (2007) as follows:

1. Knowledge societies are cultural and pluralistic.
2. Knowledge societies are for everyone and for everyone democratic societies.
3. Societies of knowledge are societies of learning.
4. Knowledge societies promote human development in its entirety.
5. Societies of knowledge are building a better future.

4.2.1. The Relations between Knowledge and Information

Knowledge is described as data by Ireogbu (2004). Because information is the communication of the idea, the facts are intended to be used to achieve certain objectives. Similarly, Garfield (1979) considers it as "facts, information, conceptions and information transmitted for the enlightenment, education and behavioral change by every accessible means to an person, groups of people and societies." The definition of Garfield was agreed by Jwakdak et al (2003) that "data is factual, heard or discussed, while Ejima (2003) views it as knowledge. The communication of understanding is therefore known as data in which "the state of understanding" refers to a "condition of understanding."

Knowledge is information and authority is knowledge. Each person or country or system's level of development and growth is mainly correlated with the appropriate data accessible to people, etc. Nigeria was among the poorest countries in the globe in terms of human growth under the UN Development Program report (2004). One might ask, how did they come to this consequence? The study indicates that understanding, that is to say adult literacy is one criterion used in the evaluation. Nigeria is only an African giant on behalf and not a human growth giant. Countries such as the USA, Britain, France, Japan and Germany, etc., are today leading the world because they know others don't know what they have and they don't. Garfield stated previously clarified that the advanced nations of the globe use data as a fundamental resource to complement domestic resources in matter and power as stated.

They spend a big part of the funds of their nation on the data scheme, according to him. What more needs we, as a country, to acquire understanding as we can in order to enter the primary stream of growth and compete with other developing countries of the globe if data is so essential for them that we are developed already.

As an instrument to acquire data and to deliver data, library is necessary. It is the only important way to gain insight. Information not adequately shared cannot transmit the understanding requested.

4.2.3. Characteristics of knowledge society

A wisdom society generates shares and utilizes expertise to help its individuals prosper and well-be. A knowledge society is believed to have the following characteristics:

1.   Their employees have achieved a greater average educational standard compared to other companies

and an increasing percentage of their workforces are employed as knowledge employees.

Fig. 1

2. Its sector generates artificial intelligence embedded goods.

3. Its private, governmental and civil society organisations are converted into smart organisations.

4. Organized understanding is improved by digitized expertise, which is stored in databases, expert systems, business plans and other media.

5. There are several expertise centers and a polycentered knowledge production.

6. There is a clear epistemic culture of the manufacturing and use of information.

7. The prices of most goods depend not on the raw materials and the physical labor required to produce them, but on the information needed for its development and sale.

8. Much of the people reach higher education.

9.   The vast majority of the population have access to ICT and the Internet.

10. Wisdom employees, who need a better degree of schooling and experience, are a significant part of the workforce.

11. Educational and research and growth invest strongly in people and the government ; and

12. Organizations must constantly innovate.

4.2.4. Indicators of knowledge society:

A series of indices have been created for the knowledge society. The most frequently used indices are:

- Qualitative use and access measurement of contemporary ICTs.
- Educational attainment;
- The number of scientists in a country;
- The quantity of research and development investment as a proportion of GDP Investment;
- Capability for high-tech production and export;
- The number of patents field in a country; and
- The number of papers in leading academic journals.

4.3. LEGAL AND ETHICAL ISSUES

Librarians and information workers also want to fulfill their tasks in an ethical manner, like all other experts. They experience many difficulties during their professional operations concerning the processing, maintenance and diffusion of data. For instance, determining whether to restrict the use of all of the computer's products in a public library, or keeping in the library a specific book that would offend some library officials' views of morality poses ethical difficulties. Charging for a government library data service enabling photocopying, preventing suspects from entering the public library–all of these examples provide examples that compel the library to decide on the basis of ethical judgement.

It is not as uncomplicated as it used to be to provide data to the correct individual at the correct moment. The development of numerous ICT instruments and methods, the conversion of the library and data landscape into a very advanced network of data and expertise and the diversification of the requirements made it hard and challenging for consumers around the world to provide data.

At the same moment, wealth development and use inequalities between wealthy and poor countries have also spread to data generation and use –leading to an "information division" between the wealthy and poor countries of data.

In his seminal article "The New World Information Order," Masmoudi highlighted the increasing worldwide inequalities in access, management, and dissemination of data.

He quoted seven major types of data inequality in the globe:

1. Flagrance in the North-South quantitative imbalance;
2. Uniform data resources;
3. A de facto hegemony and a will to dominate;
4. A lack of information on developing countries;
5. Survival of the colonial era; an alienating influence in the economic, social, and cultural spheres;
6. Messages ill-suited to the areas in which they are disseminated.

4.3.1. Factors that influence information ethics

In specific, information ethics related to the use and abuse of information, with a special focus on intellectual property, censorship, data integrity, privacy, access to information etc are the main issue for bookstores and information professionals., their professional morality as well as the application of the values to data professionals' behavior and choices have to be upheld. In the world today the areas that influence information ethics directly and indirectly are:

1. Globalization : Globalisation, characterized by comprehensive use of ICTs, a more and more open society, higher sharing of data and also higher conflict among people and cultures in asserting their domination over others is one of the most significant elements of contemporary culture.

2. More emphasis on individualism : People are nowadays more individualist; they often focus on the good of the person rather than the good of society. As a consequence, the demand for individualized and tailored library and data center services has risen.

3. Privacy and information security : The safety of personal and public data in databases, websites and repositories of other information is always at danger in this increasingly networked globe. People have become increasingly worried about their privacy and libraries as safeguards and information providers have to deal with this.

4. Diversification of 'information works' : Contradictory books and data experts today are under increasing duties, as do their predecessors. They often take on the roles of education suppliers, advisors, technology professionals, translators, synthesizers, etc., in addition to being data suppliers. They have to develop fresh abilities and capacity to carry out these tasks effectively.

5. Conflict between 'right to information' and 'ethical use of information' : There are legislation in many nations around the globe ensuring that people have the right to data (the Right to Information Act adopted in

Bangladesh in 2009). However, for security or other reasons, certain information can not be accessed by particular individuals. Librarian and data experts often have to strike the equilibrium between' limited use of data' and' right to data.' In some cases, they face difficult circumstances.

6. Access to information : Many libraries can have a problem with the problem of universal access to data. Many public and professional statements clearly refer to the freedom and access to information by all the public, as Fernández-Molina notes. For example, the code of conduct of the British Library Association states that free and public access to information should be given to any person. However, too much stress on offering a free services may lead to financial issues which could jeopardize the centre's survival. Likewise, offering service at zero price often leads to its devaluation, which also undermines the prestige and feasibility of the industry.

7. Intellectual property rights : Reproduction by photocopying, scanning or otherwise of data products has become much easier with the introduction of new techniques. Sometimes this facility hinders the rights of writers and publishers to intellectual property. It may generate a tension between data professionals 'willingness and their interest in obtaining data at the lowest possible price.

4.3.2. Ethical guidelines for information

In carrying out their tasks, librarians and informers are guided by certain moral behavior codes that encourage them to do certain things at a certain moment. A series of ethical theories have proved important to guide information professionals, such as others, through choices and action. These theories simply set requirements to distinguish between correct and incorrect behavior. Fallis describes four information theories, based on theories, duties, rights theories and virtue-based theories. Four theories deal in the field of information ethics. According to the theory based on the implications, what differentiates between correct and incorrect behavior is that they have stronger implications. We should take action that have the right consequences in order to do the right thing.

The primary idea of the duty-based theory is, therefore, that the principle that determines correct and incorrect actions should not be the result, but rather the implications. For instance, we have the obligation, although it would have very excellent implications, to avoid killing innocent individuals. The advocates of the theory of rights claim that the correct thing to do is determined by the rights of people. Such theories are very much in keeping with information ethics because debates on these subjects, such as the Library Bill of Rights of the American Library Association, are often framed in terms of rights. Ethical theorists who promote virtue-based theory believe that it is the virtues that human humans should have that that is what is correct to do. According to theories based on virtue, what is correct to do in the same conditions is a virtuous individual.

4.3.3. Legal Issue

This Declaration has been prepared for representatives of ASLIB, the Institute of Information Scientists, The Library Association, SCONUL and the Society of Archivists by the Library Association / Council for Consultation on Copyright. As the primary UK copyright voice in the library and informatic industry and in the users-the customers of data-we worry about balancing the financial rights of suppliers of data with what they need to access. This workgroup joins comparable movements in the United States, Canada and Australia to emphasize the position and needs of librarians and data workers in the digital world, particularly on the evolving highway of data.

1. General policy statement : Librarians and data

experts recognize and promote the requirements of library users to obtain data and access to copyright work, in order to help advance and disseminate understanding. They also realize that this method frequently leads to the development of fresh intellectual property. The writers, creators, publishers, manufacturers and other proprietors of copyrights respect the requirements of librarians and information professionals for a reasonable financial return on their intellectual property. We respect also their need to fight piracy, unfair use and unauthorized exploitation for copyright.

2. Rights of electronic access : The current UK Copyright Act does not, in practice, apply to electronic works, but, despite exceptions to the exclusive rights of writers in the form of fair trade, copying for instructional reasons and copying privileges given to librarians and archivists. Consequently, it is required to display, download, copy, transmit or print copyright works in digital form under agreement or under licence. We maintain that librarians and IT experts are accountable brokers and play an important role in both regulating and facilitating access to the increased amount of digital data resources, locally or remotely. Before fulfilling this task, however, it is necessary to recognize and understand its significant position in the data chain and their importance to obtain legally binding rights to all formats to use copyrighted content.

3. Information for all : Although copying certain of the information obtained from electronic sources is unavoidable, it is essential that the ideas included in published copyright works are possible for everyone to use. Both the public and the copyright owners should benefit from using and experimenting with fresh techniques. The purpose of copyright was not to avoid access to data and thoughts. Indeed, unimpeded access to knowledge, data and thoughts constitutes the foundation of democracy, and any impediment to access to it weakens the very culture that promotes the utilization of data. If, however, most of these concepts lie in digital data in future, there is a danger that only privileged individuals will be given access to payment. Except for librarians and people, there is a risk that there will be even higher divisions between wealthy data and bad data if a statutory right is given to access the use of digital data without pay for certain reasons, e.g. fair trade.

4. Document delivery : Bibliographers and users already have the technology for accessing the networks, searching information from library catalogs and databases all over the world, requesting documents and sending them to the local computer to read, store or download and print. User expect data to be rapidly accessible with the rapidly moving pace of life. The trend to make increasing data in digital form from business and non-commercial sources, optical media and networks accessible increases users ' expectations of data being provided in such a form. Bibliotecers would like thus to provide data for non-profit reasons but, because of copyright reasons, are frustrated in the effort. The library and data service can promote data flow to customers through digital access to content.

5. Lending : Loans are an significant component of the role of a librarian. Public loans are both an educational and a cultural event and should be made accessible to everyone. In the UK, government library authorities are required to provide a high-quality library service for everyone. This involves the printing and lending of other materials. Thus, audiovisuals and computer software have increasingly been added to the lending inventory, and now that libraries have become widespread with CD-ROMs and other optical techniques, they have also been loaned. Therefore, it is essential that any unfair limitations to lending are not imposed by law or by copyright owners contractually.

6. Preservation and conservation : Collecting and archiving print information for the domestic research and cultural heritage of the librarian and Archivist has always been an significant component of the role. It is also the duty of the library and data profession to keep data in similar electronic formats. To play this role it is crucial to make full use of technology. Librarians strive to preserve the long-term integrity of published media content. This is hard if the archiving of digital journals is not safe and safe from external intervention and modification. This material needs to be used in-house just as its printed equivalent if it is not commercially accessible. It is also necessary.

7. International harmonisation : We think that it is only when appropriate protection and efficient remuneration networks for use are incorporated into domestic and global intellectual property law that complete use of new technologies and sophisticated telecommunications will be completely realized. The user community is concerned that too much control could hinder access to artworks outside copyright law or which rights holders who wish to waive copyright have intentionally placed into the public domain. While it is important to protect digital work from piracy, every effort to gain control is counter-productive. Too much protection of technical copyright could discourage creativity and/or lead to copyright neglect.

4.4. INFORMATION AND KNOWLEDGE AS ECONOMIC RESOURCES

Since Plato the idea of information leadership has been around, but the riders in the last five years have brought this concept with great urgency and fresh terminology. Three primary drivers of the knowledge economy:

1. Globalization : Markets and goods are worldwide now. Worldwide renowned brands like Nike, Virgin and

Harvard. Universities now compete and work together on a worldwide scale, like other companies. Geographical limits no longer matter and as advanced nations are not competitive with manufacturing expenses, they compete in knowledge-based sectors that have significant' knowledge' and reputation.

2. Technological advances and ICT : Connectivity and networking enable the supplementation and substitution of current goods by means of the digital shipment and the creation of fresh markets by offering current goods to a much broader market via the Internet.

3. Information and knowledge : Reconnaissance of its economic significance. Every business development depends on know-how and data. About 70.0% of employees from writers to librarians, teachers to zookeepers in developing nations are skilled employees. Governments are committed to boosting economies by teaching and generating fresh opportunities through the development of information.

4.4.1. Research on the Economics of Libraries

Both its topic and strategy can define economics. Although individuals tend to think about business with regard to purchase and sale, their topic is more general cho ce: allocation of resources between competing purposes. In nearly every field of human behavior economics can and has been implemented–not only on the market, but in so many different fields like crime, marriage and discrimination, wherever individuals make decisions between competing options.

The essence of the economic approach is its assumptions:

1.   that people generally behave rationally to maximize their utility or well- being, and

2.   that they compare costs and benefits and allocate their resources, including time and money, to achieve this goal.

Trade resources on the market are one way individuals are working to boost their usefulness. Economics also assumes, in general, but not always, that the market will deliver the best possible net benefits for everybody concerned with the allotment of goods and services. Of course this description is an extreme simplification of the financial strategy. The financial strategy was defined in higher detail by Becker and MacKenzie.

Applying the financial attitude to many subjects, it has lately been applied to a subject who involves libraries and data economies.

In the word information economy, two main study fields are subsumed. One is the role of data as an input or as part of financial activity and decision making. The second is data. The other is data as a product or an output, a commodity that is manufactured and distributed. In this region, many studies focus on data services other than data itself. It comprises of implementation of financial instruments and ideas to organizations and people who generate data, associated goods and services (including libraries, libraries, publishers, and other information services and practitioners): the information and data sector.

This review focuses on the economy of libraries, which fall within the information-as-output industry of information economics. Libraries provide data facilities, not information; in other words, libraries provide access to and help with data. Library economics concerns the decisions taken within and concerning libraries. The library's objective is presumably to provide its customers with the greatest possible advantage given the resources available. It is necessary to decide which services the library will provide, to what extent and to whom; and how the library personnel, the collecting and other resources will be best allocated to these services among distinct operations. Potential consumers and financing organizations take other choices that affect the library. Customers in libraries decide whether, how much and for what purposes they will use libraries. Funders (governments, schools, universities, etc) decide how much they should spend on library facilities.

4.5. ECONOMICS OF INFORMATION

The economy of libraries is partially determined by the extraordinary nature of data. Information differs fascinatingly from most other goods. It can be sold and maintained at the same moment, for instance, because you still know what you're talking about. In addition to the use that is made of it, it is hard to value data that has distinct values for distinct persons and in distinct situations. In addition, data also has importance for individuals other than its instant customer, such as schooling for which data is often compared.

Partly due to the uncommon nature when data is sold and purchased, many data facilities are tax-supported. Therefore, the library manager turns to the economist for assistance in creating choices which could otherwise be taken by the market or by means of market data. Public funding for library services also raises questions about the appropriate role of government and private sector data service providers in providing public financing and how such services should be financed. The government support of the library services also raises questions.

This study summarizes the main applications of business theory and techniques of studies to libraries. In the space available, all the relevant research on library-let economy alone cannot be mentioned, more generally, or a historical study on data and data services economy.

This review examines the main subjects of data economics as applied to libraries and mentions significant or representative present investigations.

4.6. DIGITAL DIVIDE

The term ' digital divide' means that people who do not have access to modern technology, including telephone, television and the Internet, and who cannot make use of it, can separate the world. There is a digital divide between urban and rural regions. There is also a digital divide between the educated and uneducated, between business classes and, on the whole, between countries that are more and less industrialized.

The Digital Divide relates to the disparities in data and communication (ICT) technology (e.g. computers and the Internet) accessible and resource use and non-internet use. This involves those who do not have the skills, expertise and skills needed for the use of ICT to promote their understanding and attain their desired goals.

The digital gap according to Salinas (2003) relates to the disparity between people and/or groups able to use electronic data and communication instruments such as the Internet to improve the quality of their life and those who are not able to do so.

The word 'digital divide' has also been used for the gap between the prepared access to ICT instruments and the expertise to which and without access (Cullen, 2001) remains in most nations. (Cullen, 2001)

Deschamps (2001) claims the digital divide to constitute the increasing gap between those areas of the globe that have simple access to technological expertise, data, thoughts and data.

The divide between digital techniques and communication instruments can be described as the difference that exists between those who are able to access and do not.

4.6.1. Effects of Digital Divide

1. Economic inequality : Digital differences lead to financial inequality, since those with access to technological advances can readily collect cost-effective data.

2. Effect on training : it affects training. Students with Internet and computer access can gain more valuable Internet knowledge.

3. Democracy : the use of the Internet can contribute to healthier democracy, enhanced voter turnout and decision-making.

4. Because improved productivity tends to be associated with the use of information technologies, economic growth is caused by the digital divide, and businesses can benefit and compete better with such systems.

5. Social mobility : machines and computer networks play a part in the learning of people, in job and in the growth of the profession.

4.6.2. Factors that contribute to the digital divide

There are several factors that contribute to the digital divide. There following are some of the factors which contribute to this divide:

Gender : It has been indicated that women have less access to the Internet than men in some nations and organisations.

Physical disability : Because of technological advancements like Jaws, a multiple screen reader can use a laptop fully visually impaired and blind individuals.

Physical access : The primary obstacles in this respect are the absence of telecommunication infrastructures with enough bandwidth to provide internet and price links, the ability to buy and the needed devices. As a consequence, technology (hardware, software) is not accessible.

Lack of ICT skills and support : There are no adequate expertise in fresh contemporary technology in many disadvantaged groups.

Attitudinal factors : This stems from cultural attitudes towards technology and behaviour. Many believed that younger generations suffer from new technologies.

Relevant content : One of the reasons some individuals do not use Internet technologies because the content of these systems is not important and interesting.

Age : The latest technology appears to be a little more convenient for young individuals than for the elderly. Elderly individuals are less likely to have a laptop and less likely to use the Internet.

Family structure : Children's families have more pcs than households without, and internet access.

Motivation : Computers may not be used because they are not interested or because they see no cause to do so

4.6.3. Challenges and Barriers to Bridging the Digital Divide

Infrastructural barriers : Despite the availability of many modern and up-to-date internet and telecommunication technologies in today's world, the majority, like Bangladesh, still has little modern technology and sufficient internet bandwidth.

Language barriers : Today a significant proportion of the Internet content is in English and a barrier to those people who don't speak English in their primary language.

High cost : Because of the increased internet and technological costs, most people in developing countries are unable to use computers and internet.

Literacy and skill barriers : It is impossible to access modern literacy in a country like Bangladesh where around fifty percent are unlearned and unable to read and write, and they do not have the skill to manage technology such as computers.

Economic barriers : Lack of computer access and communication technology is also causing a digital gap. Because there is not enough money for a lower income group to spend on their own computer in cyber cafes.

Content barriers : Most of the information is published in English on the internet. Third-world peoples cannot comprehend them, so digital divide is caused. In this situation, our own content must be produced online.

Internet connectivity barrier : The high cost and absence of connectivity also because of the digital divide.

Technological barrier : People who live in village cannot get the touch of modern technology. So it also a barrier of bridging the digital divides.

Libraries, especially public libraries can play a vital role in bridging the digital divide by providing access to computer and the internet to those who do not have such facilities. Libraries are for everyone, educated and uneducated, rich and poor. So the library authority should take necessary steps to available those modern technologies and computer in their hands, and they should provide proper training to those people who do not have enough knowledge about new technology.

(i) Libraries and the Digital Divide : The library seems to reach the digitally disadvantaged, providing free public Internet access. Their only source of web access is members of disadvantaged communities who tend to utilize library pcs more frequently. In library systems and even in branches within a scheme, however, there are major disparities in the level of access. In addition, providing access to the Internet is only component of overcoming the digital divide in relation to wider social and technological inequalities.

(ii) Libraries bridge the digital divide : Because of Clinton Administration's proponents of Internet library provision, and both anecdotal and empirical evidence, public libraries have long been known as significant players in the provision of equal access to computers and the Internet, digitally disadvantaged libraries are heavy consumers of library pcs. Bibliotec bosses participate in a wide range of online operations.

(iii) Libraries as public access points for the digitally disadvantaged : Libraries have frequently championed access to public computers to narrow gaps in data. Lago (1993) asserted that public libraries were to lobby public access financing without which:

Information will certainly become a commodity for payment purposes, efficiently denying most Americans the capacity to fully achieve their potential and building two separate classes in our culture: one tiny group of knowledgeable persons and those left to their mercy.

Liu (1996) expressed this view by suggesting that the Internet could help libraries bridge data gaps between rural and metropolitan regions in particular and that Hendrix (1997) advocated the public library as a' bussing service on the [Information] Superhighway.' in particular.

4.6.4. Roles of Public Libraries in Bridging the Digital Divide

By giving computer and internet access for those who do not have such equipment, public libraries can make a enormous contribution towards bridging the digital divide. There should be an end to the perception that libraries belong to the elite of universities. Bibliothèques are wealthy and poor for all, educated and uneducated. They are equalizers and Democrat forces in computer access, learning and preparation for web data (Learning and libraries, 2004). Public libraries need to develop efficient systems for resource sharing. Because of the proliferation of data, elevated data resources costs and a decreasing library budget, any library is unable to provide its customers with all the necessary data. Therefore, the digital divide will help to meet the data requirements of customers by sharing this accessible source.

Adeogun (2003) proposed that complete access to the Internet and telecommunications device be available to the public libraries to enable them to access online data and to exchange data resources.

Second, the new knowledge economy stresses the fact that information can be transmitted from anywhere it is manufactured to where it is necessary.

4.6.5. Infrastructure for Bridging the Digital Divide

In order to ensure equal access to worldwide information in Africa, public libraries can use the following equipment and services:

1. Public internet access facilities
2. Telecenters
3. Wireless and satellite technologies
4. Mobile phone technologies
5. Information and computer literacy training.
6. Use of solar energy

4.6.6. Remedies for the Problem Facing Public Libraries in Bridging the Digital Divide

Deschamps (2003), suggested ways of bridging digital divide by calling on the UN summit on information society 2003 to:

- Commit member states to connect all their public libraries to the internet by 2006.
- Support skill development by librarians.
- Ensure that intellectual property laws for electronic publications do not prevent public access.
- Recommend public investment in information and telecommunication technologies.
- Ensure that libraries providing public access are eligible for affordable connection charges.
- IFLA president's world summit challenges were the expertise, energy and commitment of the librarians

of worldwide importance, as long as they gather the necessary resources in order to bridge the digital divide.

4.7. LIBRARY AND INFORMATION POLICY AT THE NATIONAL LEVEL

Many nations have embraced a library policy that has helped them with certain dedication and certainty to the growth of libraries. Policies also have consequences for library growth in certain industries of the domestic economy.

1. Meaning and Definition : The Library and Information Policy idea is new. New. Here we will talk about how "policy" came about in the library and information science sector. The society of today is regarded as an ICS, which at every step requires data. In contemporary culture, data in all fields of growth–social, political, economic, cultural, etc. –is regarded as a very significant source. Any nation's advancement relies upon the generation of data, its dissemination and its operation. The lack of data will have a negative impact on the growth. The need for policy is felt due to the growing request for data from all walks of life. Since the data is transmitted or distributed through the libraries, documentation centres, data analysis and consolidation centres, etc., the collection, storage and organization of data is possible. Therefore, the policy on libraries and information systems was to be formulated. The main buyers and disseminators of data are domestic governments in almost every country. Each nation should therefore develop its own domestic policy, taking account of developments at domestic and global level.

In India, an essential and harmonious aspect of social, economic, educational, research and growth, and other associated policies, formulated at multiple phases of our domestic growth, must necessarily be controlled by and be a domestic information policy. In addition, the information policy must be produced fully compatible with the country's national five-year plans.

"The national data policy is a collection of public choices to guide the harmonious growth of data transfers operations through relevant legislation and regulations to meet the information requirements of the firm. A national information policy requires the provision of tools or means essential for concrete execution, such as financial, personal and institutional. (UNISIST: Second Main Working Paper).

A national information policy would guarantee access to professional and expert information world-wide, as any country's growth depends directly on the country's government's planning and policies.

2. Library Information Policy at National Level for India : Libraries in our nation are owned and governed by a range of laws. In their growth, there is usually no coordination. Because of the following variables, library advancement was very slow:

(a) Neglect of library services during the British period

(b) Resource constraint in the post-Independence era

(c) Dependence only on government funding for the growth of libraries.

The above factors have led to the need for an integrated library or policy for India, and Dr. S. R. Ranganathan, Father of Library Science, made a first move in this direction in 1944. He proposed: "Post War Indian library building should be designed to attach main libraries to regional centers, to regional centers to temporary central libraries, to domestic center libraries of other nations and to global centres".

In order to enhance library facilities, the Government of India made numerous efforts. The Imperial Bibliothèque was renamed the National Library of India Act of 1948. The Public Library of Delhi was established in 1951. It was created in 1951 by Indian National Scientific

Documentation Centre. There was funnels for enhancement in Five Year Plans. In 1957 the Consultative Committee proposed "free to every Indian citizen" to provide library facilities.

The Raja Ram Mohan Roy Library Foundation (RRRLF) which was established in 1972 and the Indian Library Association also developed a National Library Information System Policy.

In October 1985, in order to prepare a draft document on the National Library Policy and Information System, the Ministry of Culture, Ministry of Human Resource Development, Government of India appointed a Committee of Senior Librarians and other Experts, headed in the Chair by Prof. D. P. Chattopadhyaya. On 31 May 1986, the Committee concluded its task and presented to the government a draft document.

In october 1986, the Government, under the leadership of Prof. D.P. Chattopadhyaya, appointed an Authorized Commission to implement the Committee's recommendations. In March 1988, the Committee presented its report.

The recommendations of the committee are:

(a)   Constitution of National Commission on Libraries.

(b)   Creation of All India Library Services.

(c)   Central Government's active role in the development of state public libraries.

(d)   Agencies engaged in schooling, social and rural development must also be endorsed in the growth of Public Library.

(e)   Calcutta should be reinforced by the Indian National Library.

(f)   National library system development.

3. Salient Features : A number of features that constitute the National Information Policy are given below:

(i)   Free public libraries to be established, maintained

and strengthened. A district library would become an apex library in the district, with public libraries in the city, the city and the village. They would then be in the domestic network, and each country would have its own legislation on library law.

(ii) A library and a skilled librarian should be created in all schools or colleges. Science Libraries are a key component of education in policy. A state agency should be established to properly develop state libraries at school level and a domestic coordination agency at the domestic level. The policy grants the University Grants Commission and the board of college and university libraries and states, through a memorandum of understanding (MOU, for example), that all these institutions create a network and share resources.

(iii) NISSAT (National Science and Technology Information System) expansion at domestic, regional, sectorial and local levels. The policy proposes that the NISSAT program should be further enhanced and extended at domestic, regional, sectorial and local levels.

(iv) In the social sciences, humanities and languages similar systems are structured.

(v) Informational system development and database development in various areas.

(vi) The assistance and infrastructure for libraries should be undertaken by parent bodies.

(vii) The policy proposes for national libraries comprising The Calcutta National Library, National Libraries, National Subject Libraries and National Documentation and Information Centers, National Manuscript Databases, etc. The policy proposes the national library scheme. An efficient link between all these national libraries and between books, archives and museums should be established by the National Library of India.

(viii)   Strengthening, planning and growth. The policy also proposes the use of information services by dedicated data staff which may apply contemporary leadership methods.

(ix)   Library law and information flow regulation. The policy proposes that a national library act be implemented and supplemented by models of library legislation at the state level to satisfy efficiently the evolving data requirements of society.

(x)   Use of technology. The unprecedented technological developments have undoubtedly triggered the information revolution. These advances made world data and understanding, almost from everywhere in the globe, accessible. All of these IT developments have far-reaching effects on the National Information Policy. It proposes that technology be accessed and used to enhance current facilities and to optimize the use and use of the resources available.

(xi)   Removal of communication barriers. Information, any barrier in its free flow for simple access and optimum use should be removed as a significant resource.

(xii)   National network of libraries. The National Information Policy proposes the establishment by the government of a National Library Commission and Information System. It would be responsible for the domestic network of libraries, in which books from rural society, contemporary society, schools and research organizations, would be housed at distinct rates The policy stipulates that the government of India and the state government will provide the required economic assistance of 6 to 10 percent of the systems 'education budgets.

4. Other Library and Information Policies :
UNESCO has advocated for all nations of the globe to

adopt a national (science) information policy. UNESCO has held several regional meetings and seminars in India in this respect. The NISSAT is anticipated to focus on data policies in India for the UNISIST / UNESCO programme. Significant research has been undertaken by the Society of Informatics in India to prepare the National Information Policy (Science).

There are also different associations developed at state and district level in India and other countries, for example. The Chandigarh Library Association and so on, contributing to library and information policy development and implementation for the betterment of the nation as a whole.

The policies taken in several other industries by the Government have a direct effect on the field of Libraries, such as the National Education Policy 1986, the National Book Policy 1986, Scientific policy resolution 1958, Tech Policy 1983, IT policy 2005.

The main aim of a domestic strategy is to increase the country's socialistic growth by providing all those engaged in domestic development operations with access and accessibility of data and expertise in a speedy and efficient way. Planning and programming is crucial in order to develop systematically and securely. The National Library and Information System Policy is epoch-making in the country's library motion.

A fresh stage of library growth in India is sure to come with a much better results and accomplishment if the policy suggestions are enforced faithfully. It is also essential to have a national library policy, as proposed by the advisory committee, in order to provide the library service to everyone. The Five Year Plan paid considerable attention to the growth of libraries and information technology, and the 9th Plan provided adequately. The library development will be guaranteed success when rigorously enforced.

4.8. NATIONAL INFORMATION INFRASTRUCTURE

A policy is the commitment to a generic course of action needed for the achievement of an objective which is library development in our case. The political, economic, social and cultural environment is conditional on a strategy. Policies are important in a variety of respects, such as standardizing operations, facilitating decision making, reducing confusion, coordinating different unit operations, maintaining time in training and so on. At the organizational, regional, state, national and global levels, policy declarations are to be formulated. It includes a number of fundamental problems including the growth of facilities, development of data facilities, use of new techniques, development of workforce and other overall suggestions.

REVIEW QUESTION

1. What are the challenges faces by public libraries in bridging the digital divide?

2. What are the library and information policies?

3. What are the roles of Public Libraries in Bridging the Digital Divide? Explain the perspective of Knowledge as an economic resource?

5

Communication of Channels

OBJECTIVES

The main study objectives of the communication of channels are:

- To notify scholars with the modern management principles of Information Centres and Library.

- To make conscious about the development and growth of knowledge in universities and organization in various areas.

- To offer knowledge in techniques and methods of study and their solution to the problems in Information Science and Library, preparing one for more study.

- To notify scholars with the practices and concept of Information Technology in information collection, processing, repossession and storage.

- To familiarize on the organization's principles, techniques and methods and Information centres and modern Library management.

To prepare scholars with the methods of Information Managements and provide them with the modern development in Information Technology (IT) and its application in libraries and information centres

5.1. COMMUNICATION

As a significant organizational process, academic libraries have discovered communication. Communication seems to be a significant and meaningful variable in connecting with customers of libraries and, as a consequence, involving and captivating our customers. Communication is the method of transferring thoughts, views and data from sender to receiver. In this phase, communication lines are used as a way of transferring thoughts, views and data to the recipient. Examples of lines of interaction: face-to-face, phone and e-mail. Technological innovations have brought about the emergence of a fresh medium of interaction: personal media. Social media (Twitter, LinkedIn; Facebook) are now embraced by libraries and widely adopted in communications with libraries There are serious doubts about the effectiveness of social media as a channel of communication for academic libraries, however: earlier research (Brockerhoff, 2012) shows evidence that customers are not very interested in using social media as a means of communication with the library. As a result, social media for academic libraries are not an effective communication channel. The sender's (Here: library user) signal (thoughts, views and data) will not enter the recipient (thus: database client). In addition to the use of non-customer-fit communication platforms, academic libraries strive to use a wide variety of sites. For clients, this will be complicated and can be a loss of precious library funds. The library communication method must therefore be regarded unsuccessful, hence: not lean. The lean idea (Huber, 2011) includes organisational objectives for improving client attitude.

5.1.1. Effective Communication

Communication with staff has become more sophisticated and complex in recent years. We can't just post an announcement in the staff kitchen anymore and assume the job is done. It is important that information within the library flows both vertically and horizontally. Employees are not only able to provide and receive the information they need; they are also able to trust management as well as each other. Listening has been recognized as an imperative skill that needs to be learned (and re-learned) and cultural differences add to the contest of communication. The key to good management is effective communication within an organization regardless of the means of communication or the reason for initiating it. While this requires effort, the benefits are highly rewarding.

For a multitude of purposes, we use communication every day at job, including:

- Exchanges on a daily basis
- Conditions of emergency
- Purposes of information
- Provide guidance and directions
- Coaching and praise
- Giving input and getting it
- Customer interaction
- Training
- The reproach

Communication can be as casual as a "good evening" or as official as a semi-annual conference of evaluation results. There are a range of instruments that can be used, whether official or casual:

- Conversations face to face
- Memos
- Newsletters
- Inserts for pay checking
- E-mail
- The phone

- Mail with voice
- Meetings
- There are intranets
- Instant communication and text
- Blogs

A library requires determining the most efficient techniques of communication for them. If you're attempting to hire senior from college, this individual's market may well react and favour blogs, websites, and email. On the other side, they might favour face-to-face interaction when describing a fresh strategy or operation to an senior employee. Libraries should proceed to change technology to enhance communication in attempt to draw prospective staff and meet present staff.

Furthermore, to be efficient, it is necessary to determine the most suitable interaction technique for the scenario. For instance, an evaluation of results should not be provided to a worker or performed by e-mail. E-mail should not involve private data and/or substitute the library's face-to-face discussion.

5.1.2. Promoting Open Communication

To increase open interaction within a library, the Employee Handbook may include an Open Door Policy and a Communication Policy or Statement. This will educate all staff that open communication is taken seriously by the library and value employee views.

Sample Open Door policy : Library management pursues a strategy of open doors. With your issues, questions, reviews and recommendations, your manager is the individual to turn to. He / she are accountable for your department or unit's day-to-day activities, its workload and function, payroll, personnel, and development. If you need someone else to speak to you, you are urged to plan time to share your issues and recommendations openly with the Human Resources

Manager or Library Director. We are keen in your thoughts, ideas, issues and alternatives and we appreciate the chance to share them individually with you.

Sample Communications policy : Communication between employees and management is a "two-way road." The library offers you with data and you should provide feedback and provide management with data. Our mode is casual and employees should be open to share thoughts, issues and issues with their managers or other leadership staff. Employees are urged to submit positive suggestions for activities enhancement to leadership and it is the responsibility of leadership to acknowledge and award all qualified staff whose suggestions are correctly presented and approved.

Also, in order to enhance in this region, management can (and should) participate communication and supervisory skill programs. These measures to improve interaction should create staff more ready to hear and respect leadership when communicating thoughts and recommendations regarding work.

If trust has been a problem between staff and executives in the past or if the connection of trust could use some enhancement, the following are some measures to enhance the connection of trust through interaction:

- Make your leaders stand in front of individuals. Let your individuals see leaders with candour, confidence and managing problems without fear.

- Say all the reports you've got. Say all you understand so staffs will have little room to leap to their own findings.

- Offer dialog opportunities. Message translation and analysis occurs through dialog and display, not through memos learning.

- High-tech balancing with high touch. Computers are good for quick communication, but they do not substitute conversation and debate in-person.

- Listen to your staff. The method need not be official. Simply creating the attempt will send a favourable signal.

- Communicate with each other and require more, not less.

- Remind individuals of the library's mission / vision.

- Help individuals see their responsibilities and have a favourable approach.

5.1.3. Enhancing Communication

Whatever communication method(s) your business chooses to use, there are some ways to improve the efficiency of all communication types:

Listening : This means understanding when to prevent speaking and begin hearing. This is essential when there are elevated feelings, when there is a group engaged and when there is an open exchange of thoughts. When you "hear," give close attention to what's being said and not what to write next; enable others to complete and replay what you've just been told.

Facilitating : This includes listening to what has been said, incorporating it into the subject and stating something to push the discussion forward. This will stop "running in rounds" in the discussion.

Questioning : There are many kinds of issues that can be posed for information gathering. There are locked issues requiring only a yes / no response and there are accessible issues requiring proper explanation.

Use discretion : Know when to maintain private data so that people do not lose trust.

Directing : Use to offer clear instructions so that individuals understand precisely what to do and what to expect from them.

5.2. TYPES OF COMMUNICATION

Some communication types are:

1.   According to Operating Area.
2.   In accordance with Relationship.
3.   According to Direction.
4.   Following from Mean.

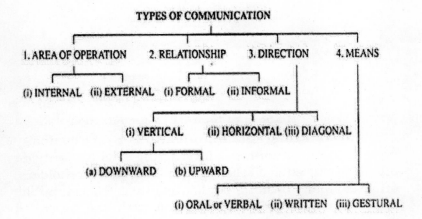

Fig. 1. Types of Communication

1. According to Area of Operation

(i) Internal Communication :   Internal Communication' is a method of communicating between the elders and subordinates or between peers or between two or more organizations within the organization. It can be official or casual, printed or verbal. As required, it can stream upwards, downwards or horizontally.

Face-to-face debate, verbal training, text, phone, intercom, meeting, conference or seminar, lecture, etc. are the oral instruments of inner interaction. Notice, manual, circular, document, chart or graph, newsletter, e-mail, fax, etc.

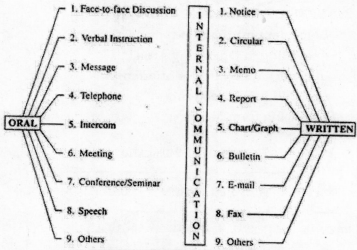

Fig. 2. Methods of Internal Communication

(ii) External Communication : A company organization requires interacting with outside organizations such as clients, distributors, shareholders, other company owners, banks, healthcare firms, public departments, etc. Such communication can be called 'External Communication' as its operating region is with individuals outside the organization.

They need to interact with overseas people, public agencies / organizations, etc. Oral internal interaction takes place through face-to-face discussions, meetings, conferences, seminars, telephones, speeches, etc. Includes notice, letter, telegram, report, e-mail, advertising, fax, press release, etc.

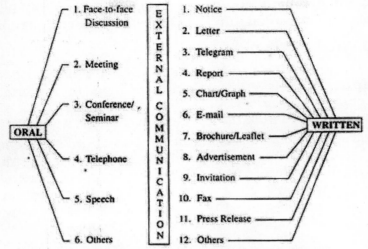

Fig. 3. Methods of External Communication

2. According to Relationship

(i) Formal Communication : 'Formal Communication' is the transfer of data or purpose in the official framework of the organization. Formal interaction retains a connection between superior and subordinate. It is an instance of formal communication when a manager directs his deputy manager to perform some task. Formal communication definitely directs employees to know what the managers intend to do and is generally codified and written in manuals, manuals, bulletins, annual reports, etc. It is therefore stiff and therefore loses the flexible value.

(ii) Informal Communication : Informal Communication' is Statement between community leaders or more than one group not on the grounds of official interactions within the organizational system, but on the grounds of casual interactions and comprehension between individuals at the same or distinct concentrations. It is called the' grapevine' indicating casual ways of distributing data or gossip. No organizational path or method follows it. It is moving in any path. It is straightforward, natural, versatile, unplanned and rapid.

3. According to Direction

(i) **Vertical Communication :** Communication flows up and down is 'Vertical Communication.' In this form of communication or data, it is transferred to the subordinates from the greater power and vice versa.

(a)   *Downward Communication :* Downward interaction implies the transfer of data or knowledge from higher-level people to lower-level people. It generally goes through printed instructions, records and manuals and is the most prevalent characteristic of all company organizations. People at lesser concentrations in the organization have a strong degree of anxiety and regard for such interaction, resulting in a strong degree of recognition.

Fig. 4. Downward Communication

(b)   *Upward Communication :* When it passes from the subordinates to the higher executives, communication is said to be upward. This classification includes submitting accounts and recommendations, views and behaviours, criticisms and grievances. Upward Communication' is less prevalent because of its troubling and perplexing complexity, it is less favoured by top executives.

Fig. 5. Upward Communication

(ii) **Horizontal Communication :** 'Horizontal or Sideways Communication' requires position at the same stage and under the same boss between two subordinates or executives. In big or decentralized organizations, it is particularly essential. Personnel assist to communicate data at the same rate between the roles and systems.

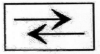

Fig. 6. Horizontal Communication

(iii) Diagonal Communication : Communication between managers or staff of various agencies is called 'Diagonal Communiqués'. No clear path is followed upward, backward, and indirect interaction requires position within it. Communication tools are used both orally and in writing. It is predominantly casual. A healthy relationship is being constructed up between subordinates and parents. It is very helpful to solve issues and avoid conflicts, but there is elevated likelihood of distributing rumours.

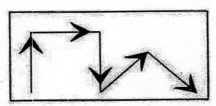

Fig. 7. Diagonal Communication

4. According to Means

(i) Verbal Communication : Verbal or Oral Communication' means that commands, instructions or recommendations are transmitted through spoken phrases. It can be face-to-face or by means of a public talking tool e.g. Telephone.

Verbal communication can move through meetings and conferences straight between one individual and another or organization or indirectly. It costs a lot of moment and allows private communication whatever instrument is used. This fosters a sense of friendliness and cooperation, guarantees fast comprehension and adequate interpretation, promotes concerns and responses, and stimulates curiosity.

Fig. 8. Verbal Communication

The speaker is also able to understand the listener's response. Again, for private and emerging discussions, it is best suited. But if the distance between the speaker and the listener is too long, it is not appropriate. It is also inappropriate if the information to be transmitted is long, reaching many people at the same time. It also lacks documented proof and potential mention and does not allow a lot of moment for the viewer to believe, behave and respond.

(ii) Written Communication : A 'Written Communication' implies a text, circular, handbook, document, telegram, department document, and newsletter, etc. for issuing a notification, command or guidance in print. It is an official communication technique and is appropriate for long-distance communication and repeated standing orders. It generates evidence records and potential references and can be sent to many people at a moment.

It provides enough moment to believe, behave, and respond to the receiver. A published communication should be evident, concise and comprehensive in attempt to be efficient. It is also time-consuming and expensive and cannot keep privacy, it provides difficulties in describing all things, it has no opportunity of clarification, it is less versatile and it is not efficient in emergencies.

Fig. 9. Written Communication

(iii) Gestural Communication : Communication can be achieved through bodily motion, face expression, smile, speech modification, gesture, handshake, hand squeezing, eye-to-eye touch, running fashion, etc. It is called' Gestural Communication' as communication is produced through movements of the body.'

Fig. 10. Gestural Communication

It should be held in mind that although communication techniques are distinct, it is not possible to use any technique alone. In order to fit the objective of the communication, distinct techniques can be used in combination.

5.3. THEORIES AND MODELS OF COMMUNICATION

In a field like Communication, theories are important

to understand because they directly impact our daily lives. The first function communication theories serve is that they help us organize and understand our communication experiences. A second function is that they help us choose what communicative behaviours to study. A third function is that they help us broaden our understanding of human communication. And the fourth function is that they help us predict and control our communication. A fifth function of theories is that they help us challenge current social and cultural realities and provide new ways of thinking and living. While theories serve many useful functions, these functions do not really matter if we do not have well-developed theories that provide a good representation of how our world works. Littlejohn considers a communication theory to be "any conceptual representation or explanation of the communication process".

5.4. CHANNELS OF BUSINESS COMMUNICATION: FORMAL AND INFORMAL CHANNELS

Various communication lines are:

1. Formal communications stream.
2. Informal Communication Channel / Grapevine.
3. Communication can also be categorized by the degree of celebration or formality it has.

Thus We Can Divide Communication Into Two Broad Categories:

1. Formal channel of communication

An official communication channel is the communication forms usually regulated by individuals in an organization's roles of power. It was therefore also related to as the' primary channel of effective interaction' of an organization.

The official interaction channel includes all the accounts, documents and other types that provide operating data to different components of an organization. These communication lines do not work automatically. A healthy organization will guarantee that they are scheduled closely and followed to their requirements.

Advantages

(i) **Effective** : The more efficient communication lines are regarded to be formal channels. With organisations expanding in volume continuously, official lines assist bridge the divide in the method of communication. It is an easy way to achieve every angle of an organization, otherwise it would be hard.

(ii) **Prevent bogging** : The guidelines are well broken down in official procedures. For instance, a employee communicates with the supervisor, the manager's supervisor, and so on. Therefore, only the data needed is processed and sent to the bottom. It stops top-level leadership from getting stuck with the meaningless nitty-gritty (practical details) of data and keeps it open for larger choices and general management.

(iii) **Better monitoring** : Formal lines can be designed by an organization to meet its particular requirements. This may assist monitor the operations of the organization. It can help to solve issues without wasting too much time.

(iv) **Good atmosphere** : Professionalism reflects good official communication lines. They assist the organization to be more strong. They also hold the managers in check.

Disadvantages

(i) **Deter free flow of information** : Formal lines prevent data from flowing freely. Formality requires only a particular path to carry the information flow. This interferes with the normal stream of data.

(ii) **Time-consuming** : Formal communication lines often result in errors. The data may not reach the individual whom it was intended for directly. It will often have to follow a circuitous official path where there may be no meaning for the interfering connections. As a consequence, official communication lines can take time.

(iii) Affects decision-making : Lower-level data filtering and tracking is a double-edged sword. Although it has its benefits, vital information may also be prevented from achieving the upper management. This can alter the view of decision taking.

2. Informal Channel of Communication / Grapevine

In an organization, the informal communication channel is often discouraged or disregarded, and is not officially sanctioned. It is known to popularly as grapevine. This is because it goes in all ways, regardless of the official framework.

The source of the word grapevine can be attributed back to the manner in which the botanical plant developed over cables, causing telegraphic signals to go unintended. Grapevine gives its presence in company lives to the gossipy nature of man.

People prefer to talk to their partners freely or lightly wherever they may be. They sense the need to be separated from the need to adhere to reasoning or reality from moment to moment.

They have informal discussion with their colleagues in the workplace as individuals go about their job. These discussions cope with private as well as company issues. This leads to the production of a rumour factory, a grapevine.

Grapevine is classified into four categories:

Single strand : Everyone is telling another.

Group or gossip chain : You tell all the people in your band.

Probability chain : Everyone tells a number of people randomly.

Cluster chain : Some say that others have been chosen.

Grapevine satisfies employees' personal requirements, contributes to more comfortable personal relationships (partially through the discharge of imagination), helps to address potential holes in formal communication and connections even those who do not fit within the official system of control.

Other characteristics of grapevine are:

(i) More people-oriented than problem-oriented.

(ii) May not be completely genuine and reliable.

(iii) Grapevine distribution passes through the organization in all ways.

(iv) Information from Grapevine is traveling very quickly.

(v) It is not possible to fix its responsibility.

Factors leading to grapevine

A rumour mill becomes active when the following factors exist in an organisation:

(i) Lack of path, particularly in moments of crises. Higher the confusion, higher the rumour.

(ii) The creation by leadership of favourite organizations of staff. This creates insecurity that leads to rumours among other staff.

(iii) Lack of employee self-confidence contributes to group creation. These organizations frequently operate rumour factories.

Advantages

(i) Speed : Speed is the most remarkable feature of this communication channel. Information can be transmitted remarkably quickly as there are no formal barriers and there is no stoppage. Therefore, a rumour can spread like a wildfire.

(ii) Feedback : This channel's feedback is much

faster than a formal communication channel. The channel is like an organization's pulse. Through this channel, the reaction to decisions, policies, directives and directives often reaches managers faster than the formal one.

(iii) Parallel function : The informal channel is not officially sanctioned, but parallel to the formal channel is unavoidable. It works as an additional communication channel within an organization. Good managers were known to use the informal channel to send otherwise unfit information to formal channels.

(iv) Support system : A grapevine is an informal support system developed within an organization by employees. It brings them closer and gives them great satisfaction.

Disadvantages

(i) Less credible : A grapevine is less believable than a formal communication channel. It can't be taken seriously because only the word of mouth is involved. Therefore, it is likely to be contradicted.

(ii) Selective information : Usually, informal transmissions do not transmit the full data. As a result, the recipient doesn't get the content of whole message. Mischief mongers or private concerns can use the medium for specific information transmission.

(iii) Creates trouble : A grapevine can cause difficulty within an organization because there is no command over the data it sends, receives, its representation and views. Information becomes corrupted. The spread of fake or wild tales can be connected with a grapevine.

(iv) Leakage : At the wrong moment, information may be disclosed. The word public secret can often be ascribed to such leaks in an organization.

5.4.1. Effective use of informal channels of communication

(i) The higher officials should guarantee that the work of the organization is well advised by the staff. This will decrease the distortion inclination.

(ii) Knowledge-updating activities should be common. This will stop rumours from being created.

(iii) There should be no favouritism from the higher officials.

(iv) The manager should meet the staff on a periodic basis.

(v) Efforts should be made by the manager to define famous staff, who can function as leader for other staff.

(vi) Employees should participate as far as feasible in the decision-making method.

(vii) Managers should not be allowed to speak as he wishes.

(viii) A manager should be a nice listener,

(ix) A manager should seek frequent feedback of his working manner.

5.5. INFORMATION TRANSFER CYCLE

Transfer of information is the method that creates, produces, disseminates, organizes, diffuses, uses, preserves and destroys knowledge.

Knowledge : Knowledge derives from an implicit hypothesis or concepts, integrated in an explanatory social context, and are supported by a practice or community of professionals.

Knowledge Creation : Externally produced, empirically grounded understanding through R&D or externally produced through R&D.

Knowledge Destruction : The unexpected or intentional information deprivation.

Knowledge Diffusion : The intentional propagation of information sometimes accidentally, particularly through personal contact. The knowledge exchange and multi-flow, Diffusion is the method through which an idea is transmitted over moment between employees of a social system through certain lines. Rogers's five-stage development propagation system comprises of consciousness, generation of concern and knowledge acquisition, development of approach, trial choice, acceptance or dismissal (Rogers, 1983).

Knowledge Dissemination : The one-way dissemination of data that enables the customer search for and obtain appropriate data outlets and discover alternatives. Another dissemination stage is interactive and gives a multidirectional stream of data into applications. To decrease expensive blindness, dissemination schemes provide data (Klein & Gwaltney, 1991).

Knowledge Management : A series of proactive operations to help an organisation create, produce, disseminate, organize, disseminate, use, preserve, and destroy information.

Knowledge Needs Diagnosis : The method comprises of meetings with clients, reflection, review of habits of use of data, and feedback from clients.

Knowledge Organization : A comprehensive data, information, and knowledge arrangement to promote identifying, access, and recovery.

Knowledge Preservation : To promote potential use, trusting retention and maintenance of papers.

Knowledge Repackaging : A system that comprises of diagnosing the data requirements of a client, consolidating and compressing data counselling. By enabling physical and visual access, it adds importance to data (Agada, 2000).

Knowledge Utilization : A method that seeks to

increase the use of information to fix issues and enhance the performance of decision-makir g in organizations. It includes developing policies that contribute to the use of information (Backer, 1991).

Organizational Knowledge : Organized business expertise through multiple entry points and technologies produced accessible to employees.

Public Knowledge : Knowledge produced through knowledge and academic and research the findings of which are produced available. Public awareness is information exchanged.

Tacit Knowledge : Knowledge in the eyes of individuals or in their own records as distinct from explicit knowledge in papers or databases. By doing this, tacit knowledge is teaching. Therefore, an organization's "major asset is knowledge."

5.5.1. Information Transfer Concepts

Definitions : Short definitions of popular words and ideas for the transition of data are as follows:

Content Management : Combining all of an organization's resources equipment, technology, individuals–to construct the website of an organisation.

Information : Data items.

Information Need : The method of becoming conscious of the importance of information.

5.6. BARRIERS TO COMMUNICATION CATEGORIES OF USERS

Research relates to the systematic technique used to define region, to define study problems, to formulate study issues, goals or hypotheses, to gather information, to analyze information and to arrive at some findings about the issue in question. In many universities in Tamil Nadu (India), study on librarianship is being implemented. The study operations also involve experts from Library and

Information Science (LIS). Researchers and scientists in Library and Information Science (LIS) need to be acquainted with and potentially pick the approaches and methods they are probable to meet as they conduct their studies.

The issue is that Library and Information Science (LIS) is a wide-ranging field using a wide range of methods and techniques. Research is not a method that is the obligation of others; study is a manner of learning, a place for each of us to make stronger practical choices" (SWISHER, 1986). He also observed that librarians can create stronger choices on how to improve library efficiency if they have understanding of the study method and are able to consume professional research literature more efficiently as people. It is further noted out by (BASKER, 1985) that librarians may need help in defining study thoughts, coaching by an skilled investigator, economic help, moment to conduct studies, benefits for timely completion of studies, aid in combining study initiatives with personal development, and motivation to submit result.

5.7. INFORMATION USE CONTEXTS

This study examines how the organisational background adds to the use of digital libraries, a data infrastructure enabled by ICT. Traditionally, the use of digital libraries is evaluated using statistical download assessment and other associated data, but statistics alone have restricted authority to describe how such a costly information infrastructure is used to satisfy organisational objectives. In this research, such limitations were achieved by related use of the digital library to the framework of such use.

Many Indian study organisations have experienced the proliferation of such data infrastructures that are immediately available to end-users over the past century. The convergence of several events such as present business models for digital assets enhanced organizational ICT infrastructure and several public measures to assist organisations make this feasible. The study was performed in two Indian research organisations in order to recognize how their corresponding environments form the use of digital libraries because of this latest change.

Two theoretical constructs were used in this qualitative survey personal agent (Lamb & Kling, 2003) and technology-in-practice (Orlikowski, 2000). Social actor's eye assisted point beyond an organization's boundaries to recognize individuals residing in its setting and generate data requirements on the organization's employees. Information requests from these organizations, which form an organisational background, often push the participants to use digital libraries.

Digital-library features therefore obtain different meanings based on the complexity and place of authority of those organizations with regard to the employees. The assumption of the other glass used–technology-in-practice (Orlikowski, 2000) is often for use in design, the centrality is not in its technical capacities, but other variables outweigh such capacities arising in a particular mode of use. In this research, this lens helped recognize several economic, technological, social, and private variables that add to digital library use habits that are very restricted.

In addition to simply evaluating uploaded information from database, the research led to our knowledge of digital library use. It extends further to explain organisational background in aspects of multiple parts and how these elements often generate employee requirements that result in digital library use. It also describes how some of the contextual elements may outweigh the technical capacities of digital libraries that lead to some traditions of use.

5.7.1. Library Context

The literature of a difficult concept of agents varies widely from "adaptable data screens" to "indeper lent programs that operate in combination with or on behalf of a natural consumer" (Adam and Yesha, p. 8Sl). As mentioned above, agents can be viewed in specific sets as software organizatious performing tasks continually and autonomously. The degree to which an officer continuously conducts his duties has consequences as to how far an agent can benefit from his knowledge. Likewise, how separately an agent do his duties has consequences for his capacity to flexibly and intelligently carry out his operations and react to environmental modifications (Bradshaw, 199P, p. P). In view of this document, officers are described as a new software category that acts on behalf of customers to discover and filter data, exchange facilities, automate complicated assignments, and work with other officers to fix complicated issues (AgentBuilder, SOOO).

We can define two kinds of public agents by assuming such a concept. The first is interaction officers that help customers primarily. These officials understand user preferences and concern with assisting consumers to fulfil their duties and dealing mainly with the screen on the computer interface of data submitted to customers. They are recognized by autonomy and teaching (Nwana and Ndumu, 1999) and are promoted as private attendants (Maes, 1994) fulfilling their duties. Examples include private news editors and data filters.

The second is data officers who undertake context duties predominantly loaded with data. They typically discover, analyze, and collect big quantities of data and mitigate overload of data (Nwana and Ndumu, 1999).

Three kinds of officers: customer interaction officers, offering a request interpreter and user profile; mediator officers, primarily serving as translators and registrars;

and officers of compilation, displaying and delivering recorded data. Agents were also used in the Zuno Digital Library (Ferguson and Wooldridge, 199P), which incorporates four agent kinds into its fundamental design: customer interaction officers, query officers, catalogue officers, and library delivery officers. User application officers record customer behaviour and private needs to enable the implementation of a variety of facilities such as customer profiling, processing of relevant feedback, searching and document analysis. User application officers operate with specialized survey officers who operate as improved query facilitators using instruments like metadata and statistical term frequency indicators, thesauri plants, and topic taxonomy plants. Catalogue agents retain information summarized and indexing services across distributed collections of libraries. Library delivery officials live on locations for the compilation of documents and manage file entry and accounting facilities.

5.8. INFORMATION SEEKING BEHAVIOUR

Behaviour requesting data is method of through series of actions to attain the required need for data. The efficiency arises when attitude and behaviour collaborate. The amount of fulfilment of the data obtained is determined based on the stage of results.

Behaviour of searching for data relates to how people search for and use data. The word was created by Wilson in 1981, on the grounds that the then present 'data demands' were unhelpful as a basis for a study strategy, since 'need' could not be immediately noted, while it was possible to observe and investigate how individuals acted in pursuing data. (The 2016 Wikipedia). Information Searching Behaviour is a wide word that includes a number of actions a person takes to connect data requirements, search for data, assess and pick data, and lastly use this data to meet their data requirements.

"The behaviour-seeking data survey can be traced

back to the early 1940s. Since that moment a big amount of research have been held out in separate areas of expertise on the distinct dimensions of data finding conduct of people. User behaviour in searching for data relies on the sort of research / study issue they are undertaking, work constraints, learning conditions, need for data, and accessibility of data references. Wilson (2003) estimated that "data behaviour includes all elements, whether effective or inactive, of individual data conduct. Behaviour requesting data is the conduct of deliberately requesting data to respond to a particular question. The behaviour of information processing is the actions resulting from the interaction of the searcher with the scheme concerned. This scheme might be a technological one, like the searcher communicating with a search engine, or a guide one, like the searcher choosing which novel is most relevant to their request. Behaviour in the use of information relates to the searcher acquiring the pattern they search" (Quoted in Gaba and Singh, 2015).

The digital environment is evolving the conduct and method of personal data. The fundamental technique of the process is usually ignored, focused almost solely on the search for and use of data, the gathering of data. As data requesting remains to move to the Internet and artificial engineering remains to promote customer conduct assessment on the Internet through a variety of customer relationships, data gathering shifts to the core of the system as applications "discover" what consumers like, want and need, as well as their usage practices (Giannini, 1998).

Research on micro-and macro-levels continues to advance across all fields that lead fresh ideas or topic regions to emerge. This generates a need to understand the data requirements of customers and behaviour-seeking data. This phenomenon thus becomes influential in carrying out on-going studies in the field of behaviour requesting data.

5.9. THEORIES OF INFORMATION BEHAVIOUR

In terms of overall policies and specific policies, library management policies can be clarified. General approaches transcend the sort of library and often include the facilities, activities and organizational buildings prevalent to most libraries; all libraries adopt these management approaches. Libraries proceed to use these management approaches as financial and data situations continue to alter, just as consumers data behaviour depends on this data. Specific libraries also implement particular environmental and library-type approaches. Besides overall policies, libraries also embrace personal approaches that match their different contexts and use them in conjunction.

5.10. ASK (AMPLITUDE SHIFT KEYING)

Amplitude change keying (ASK) is a modulation method in the framework of digital communications that imparts two or more separate amplitude concentrations to a sinusoid. These are linked to the amount of concentrations the digital message has taken. There are two stages for a binary message series, one of which is usually zero. The modulated waveform therefore comprises of sinusoid waves.

5.11. CONTRIBUTIONS OF BELKIN, WILSON, PETER INGWERSEN

Belkin, Wilson, Peter Ingwersen Contributions, Despite the mention of bibliometrics in the citation, Belkin (1990) did not present further bibliometrics.

Library and Information Science (LIS) is the research of the manufacturing of knowledge as it is materialized in records and through which means this knowledge is transmitted and how it can be accessed in terms of administration and document depiction. Studying the organisation of understanding thus performs a vital part in LIS. The organisation of information research has a lengthy tradition in LIS. However, this tradition has been defined not by a deep understanding of the nature and operates of knowledge organization in culture, but by the search for methods for knowledge association. It is therefore essential to link the research of the group of knowledge and its issues with the analysis of the creation of information by society. To understand the development of information in culture, it is necessary to recognize philosophical, his'orical, science and information sociology, cultural, literary, and social elements of knowledge production. Knowledge should not only be defined as science, but also as understanding of art, technology, and 'everyday existence'; that is a fundamental pragmatic perspective of understanding. A practical result of this concept must be to add to an awareness of why "keeping the precious out of oblivion" is essential (Patrick Wilson 1968, p. 1).

Although Peter Ingwersen is one of the representatives of information science's major officials, much of his own studies do not appear to be perceptive. For example, Serrano-López et al. (2017) is a good Wikipedia research, but it is not linked to cognitive science or the holistic cognitive perspective. As Andersen (2004, 139-144) wrote about conceptual hypothesis: "However, it is hard to see what is offered by a cognitive approach to indexing and what is behavioural about it if it provides something." Similarly, Serrano-López et al. (2017), give valuable expertise, but it's hard to see what's cognitive about it.

REVIEW QUESTIONS

1. What do you think role of communication in library management?

2. Which communication process seemed more efficient in your point of view?

3. Do you think search pattern gets changed because of digitalization?

4. What do you think about ASK (Amplitude shift keying)?
5. In your opinion what is seeking behaviour and how it is facing digitalization?

References

1. Alberti, S. (2005) 'Objects and the Museum', Isis, 96: 559-71.
2. Assam University Annual Report. (2008-09).
3. BASKER, J. What librarians need from researchers? New Library World, v.86, n.8, p.147-148, 1985.
4. Belkin, Nicholas J. 1990. "The Cognitive Viewpoint in Information Science". Journal of Information Science 16, no. 1: 11-15.
5. Bøgh Andersen, Peter and Peter Ingwersen. 1997. "Informationsvidenskab" [Information Science]. In Den Store Danske Encyklopædi. Editor-in-Chief: Jørn Lund. København: Gyldendal, vol. 9: 382.
6. Boylan, P. (1999) Universities and Museums: past, present and future. Museum Management and Curatorship, 18,1: 43-56.
7. Bradford, S.C.; Documentation. 2nd Ed., London, Croddby Lockwood, 1953, pp.50
8. Buchanan, E. A. (1999). An overview of information ethics in a world-wide context. Ethics in Information Technology, 1(1), 193-201.
9. Chuang, C. & Chen, J. C. (1999). Issues in information ethics and educational policies for the coming age. Journal of Industrial Technology. 15(4), 2-6.
10. Clifford I.B., (2014), Availability, access to and level of use of academic library information resources: study of selected academic libraries in South-Western Nigeria, Journal of Education and Practice, 5(28), www.iiste.org

11. Cullen, R. (2001). Addressing the digital divide. Online Information Review, 25(5), 311–320. doi:10.1108/14684520110410517

12. Deschamp, C. (2001). Can libraries help bridges the digital divide? Retrieved from *http://www.nordinfo.helsink.fi/publications/nordnytt/nnytt4-01/* deschamps

13. Dijk, J. V., & Hacker, K. (2001). The digital divide as a complex and dynamic phenomenon. The Information Society, 19, 315–326. doi:10.1080/01972240309487

14. Dike, V. 7th NLA conference held at Enugu (DFID) "Library for the future"2007.

15. Dr. Singer and Ms. Francisco are with The Singer Group, Inc., a Human Resources/Organization Design and Development consulting firm. They can be reached at pmsinger@singergrp.com, lfrancisco@singergrp.com, or 410-561-7561. The Singer Group's website is www.singergrp.com.

16. Dutta, S. (2003). Impact of information communication technology on society. Yojna, 47(7), 24.

17. Ejima, O.S. ICT in public Health Education in Nigeria in M.A.G (ed) Science Teachers Association of Nigeria proceeding of the 44th annual conference. Nigeria: Heinemann Educational books. 2003. Issa, A. O. (ed) libraries and librarians in the knowledge and information society. Centre for Continuing Education, the Federal Polytechnic, Offa, Kwara State. 2003.

18. Fernández-Molina, J. C. (2012). Ethical concerns and their place in the training of information professionals. Retrived on 10 April 2013 from *http://pendientedemigracion.ucm.es/info/multidoc/publicaciones/journal/pdf/ethical-concerns.pdf*

19. Garfield, E. Journal of Information Science Vol. 4:P 209 – 215.1979.

20. GOODALL, D. Public library research. Public Library Journal, v.13, n.4, p.49-55, 1998.

21. Harrington, R. (2001). "The changing face of an information vendor". Retrieved on 12/15/2017http://www.thomson.com/Investors/PPT/

22. Haywood, T. (1995). Info-Rich Info-Poor: Access and Exchange in the Global Information Society. London: Bowker-Saur.

23. Hendrix (1997Hendrix, F. 1997. Public libraries and the Information Superhighway. Public Library Journal, 12(1): 1-5.

24. http://articles.themuseumreview.org/vol1no1kozak

25. http://ebooks.lpude.in/library_and_info_sciences/BLIS/ year_1/DLIS101_LIBRARY_AND_INFORMATION_ SOCIETY.pdf

26. http://egyankosh.ac.in/bitstream/123456789/11105/1/ Unit-1.pdf

27. http://egyankosh.ac.in/bitstream/123456789/34897/1/ Unit-1.pdf, Retrieved on 12/15/2017

28. http://www.ifla.org/files/assets/literacy-and-reading/ publications/role-oflibraries-in-creation-of-literate- environments.pdf, Retrieved on 12/15/2017

29. https://en.wikibooks.org/wiki/Introduction_to_Library_ and_Information_Science

30. https://libguides.usc.edu/libsci/associations

31. https://support.office.com/en-us/article/introduction-to- libraries-23fd702b-c4ff-46e9-97dc-267d61c1249a

32. https://www.archives.gov/research/alic/reference/ archives-resources/terminology.html

33. https://www.ifla.org/files/assets/faife/codesofethics/ poland.pdf

34. https://www.wipo.int/wipo_magazine/en/2012/04/ article_0004.html

35. Ibid, p.51

36. International library statistics: trends and Commentary based on the Libecon data, by D. Fuegi and M. Jennings, June 2004. Retrieved on 12/15/2017, http://www.libecon. org/pdf/InternationalLibraryStatistic.pdf

37. Internet Encyclopedia of Philosophy (2013). Ethics. Retrieved on 12 April 2013 from http://www.iep.utm.edu/ethics/

38. Ireogbu, P. Ethics of the Teaching Profession. Vanguard Newspapers. p. 25. 2004.

39. Isaac. K. A (2014) Library Legislation in India: A Critical and Comparitive Study of State Library Acts

40. Iwhiwhu B.E. and Okorodudu P.O. (2012), Public Library Information Resources, Facilities, and Services: User Satisfaction with the Edo State Central Library, Benin-City,

Nigeria, Library Philosophy and Practice 2012, https://pdfs.semanticscholar.org/9b4a/04710e712e7b44a2bb3b95e0fd0a65237df3.pdf

41. Jwakdak, F.S et al. (ICT) (ed) S.T.A.N. 44th annual conference. Nigeria: Heinemann Educational books Pic, 61-69. 2003.

42. Kaddu, S. B. (2007). Information ethics: A student's perspective. Information Review of Information Ethics, Vol. 7 (9/2007), 1-6.

43. Khanna, J.K. (1987). Library and Society. New Delhi: Ess Ess Publications.

44. know it", Communications of the ACM, Vol. 42 No. 3, pp. 81-91.

45. Lago (1993Lago, K. N. 1993. The Internet and the public library: Practical and political realities. Computers in Libraries, 13(9): 65-70.

46. Lawrence, Gary S. "A Cost Model of Storage and Weeding Programs." College ib Research I-ibraries 42(Marc.h 1981):139-47.

47. Leslie A. Weatherly, SPHR, "Effective Employee Communication Practices for Managers," SHRM Research, Mar. 2005, www.shrm.org/research/briefly_published/Management%20Series%20Part%20III%20-%20Effective%20Employee%20Communication%20Practices.asp.

48. Liu (1996Liu, L-G. 1996. The Internet and library and information services: Issues, trends, and annotated bibliography, Westport, CT: Greenwood Press.

49. Lor P. J. and Britz J. J. Approaching Knowledge Society: Major International Issues Facing LIS Professionals. Retrieved July 19, 2012, from http://www.librijournal.org/pdf/2007-3pp111-122.pdf (2006.

50. Lourenço, M. (in press) 'University museums and collections in Europe' forthcoming conference proceedings from Atti Convegno d'Autunno dell'Associazione Nazionale Musei Scientifici, 'Il Patrimoni della Scienza, Le collezione di interesse storico' Torino, November 10-12, 2004.

51. Lourenço, M. 'Where past, present and future knowledge meet: An overview of university museums and collections in Europe', paper presented at Atti Convegno d'Autunno dell'Associazione Nazionale Musei Scientifici, 'Il Patrimoni

della Scienza, Le collezione di interesse storico' Torino, November 10-12, 2004.

52. Luhan, Hans P, "A Business intelligence system in growth of knowledge, ed. by Manfred kochen. New York, John Wiley, 1967, P. 128".

53. Maes, P. (2001), "7mart commerce: the future of intelligent agents in cyberspace", in Richardson, P. (Ed.), Internet Marketing, McGraw-Hill, New York, NY, pp. 139-4ð.

54. Maes, P., Guttman, R. and Moukas, A. (1999), "Agents that buy and sell: transforming commerce as we

55. Mai, J. E. (2016). Looking for information: A survey of research on information seeking, needs, and behavior. Emerald Publishing.

56. Masmoudi, M. (1979). The New World Information Order. Journal of Communications (Spring), 172–185.

57. Merriman, N. (2002) 'The current state of Higher Education Museums, Galleries and Collections in the UK', Museologia, 2: 71-80.

58. Morehouse, W. (1981). Separate, Unequal, but More Autonomous: Technology, equity, and world order in the millennial transition. Institute for World Order, Inc., New York, 1981.

59. Narendra Dodiya (2015) Laws, Legislation, Education and Associations (10 Pillars of Library & Information Science)

60. Nuut, Anu. (2004). "The Role of Libraries in a Knowledge-Based Society: Estonian andEuropean Experience". Diversity in Unity: Baltic Libraries in the European Union:Proceedings of the 7th Congress of Baltic Librarians, September 30 - October 2,2004, Jumurda, Madona region, Latvia.

61. Omekwu, A.Organization of School Library Materials at a Period of Economic Difficulties: A Paper Presented at the 23rd Workshop for Teachers Librarians in Abakiliki Zone. 15 – 16 June.2005.

62. Orlikowski, W. J. (2000). Using technology and constituting structures: a practice lens for studying technology in organizations. Organization Science, 11(4), 404–428

63. Palmour, Vernon E., et al., Costs of Ownzng, Borrowing,and Dzsposing of Perzodzcal Publications. Arlington, Va.: Public Research Institution, 1977.

64. Peter D. Sustainable Globalization? The Global Politics of

Development and Exclusion in the New World order. In Allen, T and Thomas, A (eds) Poverty and Development in the 21st Century. London: Oxford University Press.1969.

65. Ranganathan, S.R. (2016) The Five Laws of Library Science: Ess Ess Publication

66. Ranganathan, S.R. Documentation and its facts, Bombay Asia Book House, 1963, p.46

67. Rawson, H. (2004) "'I observed nothing remarkable": the presentation of, and responses of visitors to, objects of significance at the University of St Andrews, from 1677', paper presented at University Museums in Scotland Conference 2004: The Significance of Collections, November 12, 2004.

68. Rosenbaum, H. (1993), Information use environments and structuration: towards an integration of Taylor and Giddens. In S. Bonzi, (Ed.), Proceedings of the 56th Annual Meeting of the American Society for Information Science Vol. 30 (pp.235-45). Medford, N.J.: Learned Information

69. Shari Caudron, "Rebuilding Trust Through Communication," Workforce Management Research Center, Oct. 2002, www.workforce.com/archive/feature/23/33/47/ 233349.php?ht=non%20verbal%20communication% 20non%20verbal%20communication.

70. Smith, A. (1980). The Geopolitics of Information: How western culture dominates the world. London: Faber and Faber.

71. SWISHER, R. Focus on research. Top of the News, n.42, p.175-177, Winter 1986.

72. UNESCO Towards Knowledge Societies UNESCO World Report. Paris: UNESCO. Retrieved August 4, 2012,from http://www/unesco.org/publications.2005.

73. Venkatappaiah V. (2015) Indian Library Legislation: State Library Bills & Acts

74. Warhurst, A. (1986) Triple crisis in university museums. Museums Journal, 86,3: 137-140.

75. Warwick C., Terras M., Galina I., Huntington P. and Pappa N. (2007), Library and information resources and users of digital resources in the humanities, http://discovery.ucl.ac. uk/13807/1/13807.pdf

76. Watson Wyatt, Connecting Organizational Communication to Financial Performance—2003/2004 Communication ROI

Study, www.watsonwyatt.com/research/resrender.asp?
id=w-698&page=1.

77. White, Ben (2012). Guaranteeing Access to Knowledge: The
Role of Libraries. WIPO Magazine, Retrieved on 12/15/2017,
http://www.wipo.int/wipo_magazine/en/2012/04/
article_0004.html>.

78. Wiedrrkehr, Robert R. V.Alternatzves for Future Library
Catalogs: a Cost Model. Rockvillr, Md.: King Research, Inc.,
1980.

79. Wilson, Patrick. 1968. Two Kinds of Power: An Essay on
Bibliographic Control. Berkeley, CA: University of California
Press.